The Antiquities of Jordan

The Antiquities
of Jordan

G. LANKESTER HARDING

Thomas Y. Crowell Company

NEW YORK · ESTABLISHED 1834

The translation of the Moabite Stone, on pages 26, 27, is reprinted from *Ancient Near Eastern Texts Relating to the Old Testament*, edited by James B. Pritchard, by permission of Princeton University Press.

In the caption for Plate 5 (c),
the plan referred to appears on page 44.

Designed by Laurel Wagner

Library of Congress Catalog Card No. 60-6232

Manufactured in the United States of America by the Vail-Ballou Press, Inc., Binghamton, N. Y.

Halftone illustrations printed in Great Britain

For A. H. M.
In gratitude

. . . for there are rest and healing
in the contemplation of antiquities.

Introduction

To HAVE SPENT twenty years in Jordan, as I have, does not make it easy to write a good book about it; intimate acquaintance with a place for a long period of time inevitably eradicates the impressions of its first impact unless one keeps a diary, and that I have never done. Likewise with time one begins to forget what the place as a whole looks like as one concentrates on the details which make up the picture. As I first went to Jordan in 1932 and took up residence there in 1936, time has had ample opportunity to get busy on my vision of the country, and the large view has been submerged in the fascination of minutae. On my first visit I went more or less as a tourist, taking a busman's holiday with other members of the expedition at the end of a season's excavation with Sir Flinders Petrie at Tell al Ajjul in South Palestine. Some sites visited then for the first time—such as ancient Jericho—seemed very dull, but have since become of absorbing interest, while others, such as Jarash, were overwhelming in their first impressions but had not much to offer for subsequent investigation. It naturally never occurred to me then, as I looked for the first time at the ruins of Jarash and Petra, that I should one day be responsible for the preservation not only of such outstanding sites but also of all the thousands of other ancient remains in East Jordan.

But when I returned in 1936 it was as Chief Curator of Antiquities, a title subsequently changed to Director, and fortunately for my peace of mind I could not foresee just how much I had in fact taken on. For in 1948 a large area of Palestine also came within my area, and this ultimately included the great problem of the Dead Sea Scrolls, which has occupied much of my time and energy during the past few years. Before 1948, however, existence was more leisurely, and I have been able to visit most corners of Trans-Jordan, as it then was, chiefly by car in my faithful Ford V8, bought new in 1936 and still going strong when I left in 1956. My equally faithful and indeed indispensable companion on all these trips was Hasan Awad, whom I had first known as a small boy aged about thirteen or fourteen in 1926, and who had grown up in archaeology. He has a remarkable flair for it and a very sharp eye for ancient remains; many a prehistoric site was first discovered by him. He is also one of the finest excavators I know, with a delicacy of touch and a patience that must be seen to be believed, and great ingenuity in overcoming difficulties of all kinds.

This book was actually started some years ago and was intended solely as a guide to the principal ancient sites likely to be seen by the average visitor, together with a little information about the country and its history. For apart from Baedeker and the *Guide Bleu* there was no volume which covered the whole country in a general way, and that there was a demand for such a work was clear from the great number of tourists who asked me what they could read when visiting the country. But it has now been largely rewritten and recast in the hopes of its being of some interest to the arm-chair traveller as well as of practical use to the visitor on the spot. Attention has been confined chiefly to East Jordan, as there are many good books already in existence about the West, or Palestine, side, but in view of the importance of recent work and discoveries in the Jericho neighborhood I have included a chapter on that. Dr. Kathleen Kenyon's work at ancient Jericho and Père de Vaux's work at Qumran and on the Dead Sea Scrolls are both world famous now; and, although on the latter subject many hundreds of books and articles have already appeared, I felt it should not be omitted from a work of this nature.

It had also been my intention to begin with a chapter of general information on the country, but I soon had to abandon that idea, for conditions changed—and are still changing—almost from week to week, and statements about them would be out of date before even the type could be set up. And I had planned to give road distances and times between the various centers and the sites, but again new roads are being laid down everywhere, many of which were not finished when I left in 1956, and it was useless to give these details which applied to the days when most of the roads were really no more than roughly surfaced tracks instead of the excellently made and surfaced highways many of them are today.

There are, of course, hundreds of ancient sites which do not even get a mention here, but they are the sort of places which are of interest only to the archaeologist, for they are generally rather difficult to get at and in most cases nothing but a few potsherds are visible on the surface. With the increased tempo of travel in these days, visitors tend to spend less and less time in one country and only want to know what they can see in the shortest possible space of time. So I have concentrated on the most impressive, interesting and easily accessible sites, and indeed there are more than enough of these; few countries can boast of two such unique sites within their boundaries as Petra and Jarash.

Every writer of a book of this kind owes an immense debt to the travellers and scholars who have gone before him, and I am no exception. I am further indebted to many who read the manuscript in both its original and recast form and made most helpful criticisms and suggestions. My most sincere thanks go to Miss Gwendoline Brocklehurst, who typed the whole thing in her spare time. And I cannot omit mention of the encouragement of the publishers.

Limassol.
1958.

ACKNOWLEDGMENTS

The author and publishers wish to thank the following for permission to reproduce the plates of which they hold the copyright: the Department of Antiquities of Jordan (Plates 1, 2, 4, 5, 6, 7, 8, 9, 10 (a), 11, 12, 13 (a), 14, 15, 16, 17, 18, 22, 23, 24, 29 (a); with the exception of Nos. 1 and 17, all these photographs were taken by R. Richmond Brown, F.S.A.); the Palestine Archaeological Museum, Jerusalem (Plates 3, 13 (b), 19, 20, 21, 27, 28, 30, 31); Dr. Kathleen Kenyon of the British School of Archaeology in Jerusalem (Plates 25, 26); The Shell Petroleum Company Ltd. (Plate 10 (b)); and the Radio Times Hulton Picture Library (Plate 29 (b)).

Contents

xii

Illustrations

xiv

B The finest Neolithic plastered skull, after conservation.
This is one of the unique finds made at Jericho

27 Khirbat al Mafjar
A The entrance to the vast Umayyad palace
B One of the superb mosaics

28 Khirbat al Mafjar
A The floor of the baths is one of the largest single areas of
ancient mosaic so far discovered
B A superb example of the carved stucco from the baths

29 A Khirbat Qumran. Cave I, with the two Taamirah Bedu
who first entered the cave
B The author sorting fragments of Dead Sea Scrolls in the
Palestine Archaeological Museum

30 An aerial view of Qumran showing the settlement of the
Essene sect

31 Khirbat Qumran
A A view of the settlement from the western scarp with the
Dead Sea in the background
B The caves where some of the Scrolls were found
C Cistern steps showing the effect of the earthquake of
31 B.C.

PLANS AND MAPS

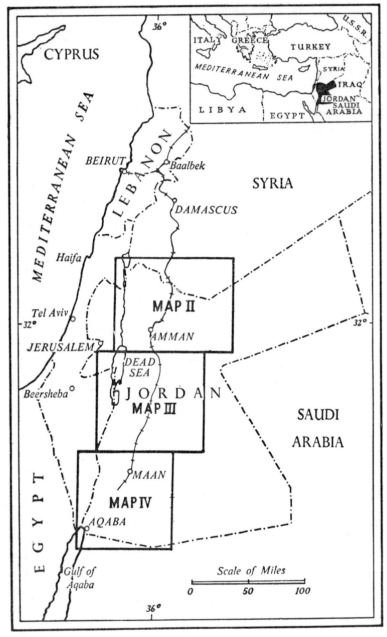

Fig. 1. Key map of Jordan and neighboring countries. Details of insets will be found on the following pages: Map II on page 39; Map III on page 91; Map IV on page 122.

Chapter I

JORDAN: TOPOGRAPHY · CLIMATE · NATURAL HISTORY · THE INHABITANTS · DEPARTMENT OF ANTIQUITIES

EAST JORDAN presents many varieties of scenery, ranging from dreary black basalt wastes with scarcely a sign of life in them to beautiful green valleys with clear running streams bordered with oleanders; and from the flat, colorless monotony of the desert to the brightly colored sandstone mountains of Rum. Yet even the basalt country is not without charm, and there are many who fall in love with the quiet and stillness of the desert. But likes and dislikes in the way of scenery are so very personal and individual that no amount of recommendation or eulogy of a particular spot is likely to have any influence. All that can be done is to try to indicate what is there, and leave it to the visitor to make his choice.

For descriptive purposes, the country can be divided into two main sections, a rough boundary between them being the railway line running north and south. The narrow western strip is mountainous but fertile; the eastern section is a flat plateau, with the desert and the basalt country.

The mountains of the western part run in an almost straight line along the border of the Jordan valley, the Dead Sea and the Wadi al Arabah, from the Sea of Galilee to Aqaba. The range is divided into sections by some fairly large perennial streams, the names of which from north to south are: Wadi Yarmuk, Wadi al Zarka (ancient Jabbok), Wadi Shaib (beside which runs the Jerusalem-Amman road), Wadi al Mojib (ancient Arnon) and Wadi al Hasa (ancient Zered). The first three flow into the

Jordan, the last two into the middle and extreme southern end of the Dead Sea respectively. There are a few smaller streams, such as the Wadi al Yabis, Wadi Nimrin and Wadi Hasban, while the Mojib has a fairly large tributary in the Wadi Wala. Also there are hot mineral springs at Zarka Main near Madaba and at Hammah in the Yarmuk gorge; these are popular health resorts at certain seasons of the year. All these valleys with permanent water are green and pleasant to the eye, as the sound of the stream is grateful to the ear, and in the springtime, from mid-January to March, the mountainsides are covered with wild flowers of many kinds.

From Yarmuk to the Hasa the mountains are of limestone, and their tops are smooth and rounded; between the Yarmuk and the Zarka they are covered with forests of small scrub oak, and in the Ajlun district there are some fine pine forests. On the road between Jarash and Husn is a large solitary tree, last remnant of the forests which, up to the time of the First World War, covered this district. The tree is a sacred one, and wishes are addressed to it accompanied with the tying of a piece of rag to a branch, but whether it has survived because it was sacred or has become so because it has survived cannot be ascertained.

From the Hasa southwards there is a gradual change from limestone to sandstone, the hills taking on a jagged outline, and the scenery becoming wilder and more exciting. In the extreme south, around Aqaba, are granite, basalt, shale and other igneous rocks; garnets are found here, and sometimes turquoise and amethyst. On the western slopes of these mountains, in the Wadi al Arabah, are deposits of copper and iron which were worked in ancient times. The ore is still there, but in such small quantities that the mining of it would not be a commercial proposition today, particularly with the great difficulties of transport involved. There are also very small deposits of other minerals, such as manganese, in this neighborhood, while at Rasaifah near Amman there are considerable phosphate deposits which are being exploited, and at Qasr Hamman, east of Zizia, are hills of colored marble, red, blue and green, the cutting and polishing of which now forms a large local industry. In the Mahas neighborhood west of Amman is found kaolin (china clay) and ochre.

In the western strip is all the cultivation of the country, vineyards and cornlands, and all the large towns and villages. There are but very few permanent settlements east of the railway, and likewise very little agriculture, though with the peace and security of the past twenty-five years there has been a steady extension eastward, and areas of desert which have never been cultivated before are now under corn.

Of the eastern section there is not much to be said. The northeastern corner is the lava and basalt country, black and rather grim, which stops abruptly at Azraq at the head of the Wadi Sirhan, the flat valley which runs down into Saudi Arabia. At Azraq itself there are considerable stretches of permanent water, where in their season you can see all manner of wild birds. There is excellent shooting to be had—duck, snipe, goose, teal, etc.—but development projects are in hand, and the birds are not so numerous as before. Here begins the rolling desert, its surface covered with flint and limestone flakes burnt dark brown in the sun of thousands of years. This type of country continues southwards until it ends rather abruptly at the sandstone mountains of Jabal Tubaiq.

The climate is variable and healthy, there usually being at least one fall of snow during the winter, and temperatures running up to 106° F. in the summer, though the average is about 86° F. Touring the country in summer is not, on the whole, to be recommended, for it is hot and dusty, without much green vegetation to relieve the monotony of the brown landscape. The rainy season starts with an occasional shower during November and December, then heavy rains, sometimes falling for three or four days without a break, occur in January and February, followed by a gradual easing off in March and April. These two latter months, despite the possibility of rain, are the best for travelling, but it must be emphasized that it can be extremely cold even then, and thick coats are a necessity. A snowstorm has been known at Petra even in mid-April, but that was

3

definitely exceptional. The peculiar geographical position of the Jordan valley makes Jericho an ideal winter resort, it being nearly always warm and sunny there.

The country is singularly free from noxious insect pests, and even during spring the visitor will find but few mosquitoes and sandflies; he may collect an odd creepy-crawly or two in the course of his travels, but they do not constitute a serious menace, and stories of their ferocious habits should be taken with a few grains of Dead Sea salt. The periodic invasions of locusts are an amazing sight if you should be unlucky enough to run into one, but they would not in any way incommode the traveller. There are not many varieties of snakes, and only two of them are really poisonous, the ordinary viper and the horned viper; the latter is dangerous, but fortunately confines his habitat to the desert parts and is seldom seen in inhabited areas. Scorpions, both black and yellow, are not uncommon, but a sting usually does no more than give an unpleasant twenty-four hours. The same applies to the large yellow-and-blue centipede, and if you should find one of these walking up you, be careful to brush it off the way it is walking, otherwise the sharp legs are apt to dig into the skin and cause an intense irritation.

The wild flowers which burgeon everywhere in the spring transform the country for a few weeks into a vast natural garden, which has to be seen to be believed. Perhaps the most characteristic flower is the black iris—really a very, very deep purple —which grows in profusion in the hill regions and is particularly noticeable in the plain between Amman and Zizia. Red anemones, anchusa, cyclamen, hollyhocks, tulips, annual chrysanthemum, fritillaries and asphodel are among the most "profuse bloomers," as the seed catalogues have it, and until recently the fields of wild blue lupins in the Wadi Shaib were a famous sight, although they have now mostly been plowed away. The valleys and plains —even the desert in a good rainy season—are carpeted with intricate patterns of blue, red, yellow and purple on a background of green and brown. It sounds crude in writing, but in actual fact is quite enchanting. Among the shrubs, the pink oleander fringes the banks of every little stream, gorse grows in the moun-

4

tains, and white broom flourishes everywhere, but is particularly striking in such places as Rum, where the bushes sometimes reach such a height as to hide a man on camel back, and the air is sweet with the scent.

The fauna, being mobile, is much more elusive; none the less it is quite likely a few jackals and a fox or two can be seen running across the road in front of the car or making off across the fields. Wolves, hyenas, martens, mongooses and the like are very rarely seen but are fairly common, as are also hares (but no rabbits). Gazelles were once prevalent in all parts of the country, but the growth of the villages and the advent of the motorcar have driven them farther out into the desert, where they wander about in herds of twenty or more, though as a result of being hunted in jeeps they are retreating ever farther eastwards. In the Hasma area to the south of Maan, and occasionally in the hills around the Dead Sea, there are still a few ibex, even an occasional leopard; also wild cats and coneys. Bird life is abundant and various, and there are some beautiful and interesting migrants in spring, such as the golden oriole and the storks, which come over in great clouds of seven hundreds at a time. In Petra and its neighborhood is a lovely rose finch, the brightly colored rock thrush, and Tristram's grackle. In this part also can be seen sky-blue lizards, and others with red or blue heads; their presence has nothing to do with sobriety or otherwise. Until about twenty-five years ago ostriches were still found in Jabal Tubaiq, but they have now retreated to the fastnesses of Saudi Arabia.

Occasionally a remarkable phenomenon can be seen in the desert, parts of which receive rain only once every two or three years. When it does come it is usually in a downpour, and small, shallow pools are rapidly formed which last, perhaps, for three or four days. Within a short time of the pool's forming it becomes alive with tiny creatures swimming about busily on their affairs, as if they had never known any life except in water. During the brief free-swimming time allotted to them they mate and reproduce, and the offspring bury themselves in the mud at the bottom of the pool, there to await the next rains, when the cycle will be repeated. It is astonishing that they can survive

5

so prolonged a period of drought and work their way through to the freedom of the water so quickly.

As for the human inhabitants of the country, they are of two main types, and again the railway forms a rough boundary, from which fact we can deduce the modes of life of the two sets of people.

The eastern section is occupied almost entirely by the people we know as the Bedu or Bedouin, though they call themselves "The Arabs" ('arban); in this they are being purist, but perfectly correct. The Bedu are the true Arabs, having racially little in common with the peasants and villagers, which latter are probably, however, the older inhabitants of the country. Indeed, quite apart from some slight variation in dress, the physical differences are obvious to anyone with an observant eye: the narrow, lean face, bright eyes and sparse build of the Bedu, and the round, complacent face and stocky build of the Fellah or peasant. Statements such as this are, of course, no more than generalizations and exceptions will be found on both sides.

The Bedu are originally nomads, each tribe wandering within its own tribal boundaries, but they are now rapidly becoming settled and encroaching upon the western section. This generally brings about a certain amount of decadence as they breathe the more sophisticated air of the town or village, even though in some ways they may become more useful members of the community. But they never lose either their great hospitality or their beautiful manners, which have justly earned them the epithet of "Nature's gentlemen." They live in tents of goathair cloth, woven in long strips and sewn together by the womenfolk, and their main livelihood is the raising of flocks and herds of goats, sheep and camels, and with some tribes the breeding of fine horses, though with the advent of the motorcar the demand for both camels and horses has dropped considerably. The animals and their owners move from pasture to pasture, and in the summer sheep and goats can be seen in the desert busily nibbling away at, apparently, the flint and limestone flakes, for little else is visible.

By nature the Bedu are intensely independent and individualis-

6

tic, resenting any encroachment on their freedom. The order of their loyalty is first their immediate family, then the wider family, then the tribe. If the tribal leaders give their allegiance to a still higher ruler, then the tribe will follow their lead. But this independent outlook has prevented them from ever molding themselves into a coherent whole for the attainment of any specific object, even under the most inspired of leaders.

Their life is simple, hard, and on the whole pleasant, though there are many who sigh for the "good old days" when raiding parties used to dash about the countryside with a great deal of noise and not much real danger, and one never quite knew who was going to turn up next. Raiding each other was, indeed, the Bedu's chief pastime, but the "ghazu," as it was called, has been entirely abolished in Jordan, and the last tribal raid took place in 1927. They are still allowed to carry arms, rifles, revolvers, swords and daggers, and are none the worse for it; each man is thus his own policeman, and crime is reduced to a minimum. They have their own set of laws and tribal courts, and are normally quiet and law-abiding. A number of Negroes are to be found among the tribes; these are the descendants of slaves who have become completely Arabicized and are accepted as members of the family, except that there is no intermarriage so far as the Negro males are concerned.

The other section of the population is now, and probably always was, very mixed. First there are the native Fellahin or peasants and farmers of the country; they are most probably the descendants of the Edomites, Moabites, Amorites and Ammonites of the Old Testament, differing little in general mode of life from their ancestors. Like the peasants of most countries they are pleasant, hospitable, suspicious, gullible and slightly boneheaded; like their counterparts elsewhere they are the real backbone of the country, for such natural wealth as Jordan has lies entirely in agriculture. They are, however, avid of improvement in their husbandry, and have taken eagerly to motor tractors, harvesters and reapers, and other mechanical aids to farming. But in their home life they are more conservative, and the plan of an average small peasant house could be duplicated in

7

almost any excavation of an ancient site. And good it is that they retain their traditions, for a people who discard them discard the very basis for their future advance and improvement.

In the northern districts there are settlements of Circassians, Chechens (much the same as Circassians) and a few Turkomans; also a sprinkling of Druses and Persian Bahais. All these are fairly recent arrivals, the first three having been settled here by the Turks towards the end of the nineteenth century. Circassians are to be found chiefly in Jarash, Swailah and Wadi Sir; they are all bilingual, speaking their own language and Arabic with equal ease. In Turkish times they also spoke Turkish, but nowadays most of them have English as their third tongue. The latest generation are almost indistinguishable from their Arab neighbors, for there has been much intermarriage as the Circassians are Muslims—the reason they were persecuted in Russia and fled to Turkey. The royal bodyguard is composed entirely of mounted Circassians in their traditional dress, and very fine and imposing it is. The Turkish tradition of the fair, surpassing beauty of the Circassians has not been borne out by those I have met, but perhaps I have just been unlucky.

The townees—shopkeepers, mechanics, clerks—are mostly Syrians and Palestinians, and a large proportion of the Fellahin and Bedouin are born and die in debt to them. The arrangement does not, however, seem to cause any sleepless nights or to bring about disaster for either party, except very occasionally; debt is contracted with a light heart and a mental reservation that it will almost certainly not be paid in cash. The shopkeeper is fully aware of this reservation and quite prepared to take payment in kind, which can always be converted into cash. These remarks, of course, apply only to the small fry; in cities such as Amman and Irbid big business is now the order of the day.

Islam is the state religion of Jordan, but there is also a small Christian community there. These latter have lost nothing of their Byzantine ancestors' passion for church building: a comparatively small village like Husn boasts seven churches. Perhaps this is not quite comparable to sixth-century efforts, when there was only one sect—Greek Orthodox—in the early period, whereas

8

nowadays seven churches probably represent seven different sects.

As this is a book primarily about the antiquities of Jordan, a word must be said about the government Department of Antiquities. The Jordan Archaeological Museum, which is the headquarters of the department, is situated on Citadel Hill of Amman and houses a collection of objects illustrating the life and history of the country from prehistoric times to A.D. 1700, at which date objects officially cease to be antiquities. The chief function of the department is administrative, to prevent damage to the many ancient sites in the country, and to carry out such works of conservation and excavation as become necessary from time to time. There are many fine monuments to the country's ancient culture, such as Petra, Jarash, Umm al Jamal and some fine Umayyad castles, as well as hundreds of less spectacular sites which are equally, if not more, important archaeologically.

An Antiquities Law has been framed to cover all aspects of archaeological activities, a very important one being the prevention of illicit digging, which destroys not only ancient objects but also their whole archaeological and historical value. In this work every visitor to the country can and should help by refusing to buy antiquities offered them casually in the course of their travels. A demand will always create a supply, which can only be obtained illegally. The department itself offers for sale a small quantity of antiquities—lamps and coins, for instance—which have the advantage of being unquestionably genuine, which cannot always be said of the merchandise of dealers. If, however, you are offered something outside which you simply cannot resist, do please show it to a responsible official of the department, either in Amman or Jerusalem, before taking it away and preventing an assessment of its archaeological value. It might be of considerable interest and importance, in which case the department would like to have a record of it, for it might well lead the expert to further discoveries.

Chapter II

In COMMON with all other countries of the Near East, Jordan has been occupied by man since the earliest prehistoric times. The country never, however, enjoyed the high degree of wealth and civilization attained by its neighbors, Syria, Iraq and Egypt, the chief reasons being its geographical isolation and lack of any large natural sources of wealth. On the west the Jordan, Dead Sea and Wadi al Arabah effectively separate it from Palestine; on the east are the great desert wastes, and on the north, where it might have merged into Syria, the gorge of the Wadi Yarmuk makes a natural boundary. On the south the boundary is more open, though the desertlike nature of the country does not make communications particularly easy.

Nevertheless, despite this lack of close and direct contacts, there is ample evidence of both Mesopotamian and Egyptian influences. These arrived chiefly via Syria and Palestine respectively, probably already somewhat distorted; some Babylonian influences even percolated through Arabia. The ordinary objects of ancient everyday life, such as the pottery, though very closely resembling those of the most intimate neighbor, Palestine, have certain peculiarities of detail which show their native individuality. And with the Nabataeans Jordan produced a culture which, by the style of its work, can be recognized anywhere (Plate 17).

Comparatively little excavation has as yet been done, and the chief sites examined cannot be considered as typical of East Jordan. Tell al Khalaifah, near Aqaba, was a smelting site and almost an international port, the Ezion Geber of the Bible; Talailat Ghassul in the Jordan valley—and any other sites there —is more closely related to Palestine than the sites in the mountains. Jarash, where an American expedition worked for some years, represents only the Roman and Byzantine periods, when individuality had largely disappeared, and within the Roman Empire living conditions were fairly standardized. The excavations at Petra and Khirbat Tannur in the Wadi Hasa represent the Nabataean culture, and at Wadi Dhobai in the eastern desert a prehistoric site has been examined. In fact, the only really typical Jordan site so far excavated is Dhiban, the Biblical Dibon, and this proved dissappointing, as each succeeding peoples re-used the building stones of their predecessors and so destroyed the hoped-for stratification. Some work has also been done on the citadel at Amman by an Italian expedition, but here nearly all the early remains were cleared away by the Romans; at Adar and Balua in the Kerak district some work was done by English and American societies, but up to date only the most meager reports have been published of the results of these last three expeditions mentioned, also those of Khalaifah and Tannur, and so far as the elucidation of Jordan's history is concerned the work might never have taken place. The greater part of the country is still untouched, and is a promising field for investigation; the fact that such important things as the Balua stele and the Mesha stone (see pages 21–22 and 92–93) have been found casually gives an indication of what might be revealed by controlled scientific work.

In remote geological times parts at least of East Jordan were under the sea, for fossilized oyster and other shells are found in many parts of the country, and the phosphate deposits at Rasaifah near Amman contain the bones and skeletons of many kinds of fish, giant lizards and turtles of about eighty million years ago. There were vast periods of time during which occurred extreme fluctuations of climate and rainfall, and immense volcanic and earthquake action was constantly changing the contours and appearance of the country. It must always be borne in mind that geological periods run into millions of years, historic periods only into thousands.

Palaeolithic, c. 200,000–8000 B.C.

By the time Palaeolithic man appeared on the scene, conditions must have been very much as they are now. The large, boldly flaked flint implements called hand-axes, associated with the early palaeolithic culture, are found scattered all over the country, for man was not yet a social animal and lived only on what grew of itself or what he could catch with his hands. In the earliest times he did not, apparently, even live in caves, but wandered over the face of the earth like the other animals.

In time a wide variety of implements were devised—scrapers for cleaning skins, points for drilling and boring, knives for cutting, and the large flaking of early days very gradually gave way to finer and more delicate work. Development was very slow indeed, there being little change for some 150,000 years, but by the end of the Palaeolithic period an artistic sense was developed, and at Kilwa in the Jabal Tubaiq, the southeastern corner of the country, there are scratched or hammered on some rocks outlines of various animals then extant. An interesting feature confirms the very early date of these drawings, in addition to the presence of many flint implements. Superimposed on some of the figures are Thamudic inscriptions, of about the fifth or sixth centuries A.D. and these inscriptions, after exposure to the sun for some 1,500 years, are still white, whereas the drawings of the animals hrave been patinated a dark brown, indicating an exposure many times as long as that of the inscriptions.

Neolithic, 8000–4500 B.C.

In this period implements of very great delicacy and considerable beauty were being made, and another technique, that of polishing the cutting edges of axes, was evolved. Also by now man had settled down to a social life, living in huts and villages. Recent excavations at Jericho have shown us that, in fact, this was a period of far higher culture than we had hitherto suspected, for here was not merely a village of well-built houses with fine plaster floors, but there was a great stone wall all round the settlement with a ditch or dry moat in front of it. This implies a high degree of communal organization, of subordinating the personal interests to those of the many. Further, a magnificent circular stone tower with a shaft down the middle in which are well-made steps, shows a high degree of architectural ability (Plate 25B). It would almost seem that in the Jordan valley at least, earliest Neolithic man was culturally well in advance of the surrounding countries.

Artistically, too, these people were well advanced, for we find almost lifesize human figures made of lime plaster, curiously thin and flattened, with hair and other features painted on, and the eyes made of inlaid shells. Another remarkable find at Jericho was a series of skulls, on which the facial features had been modelled in lime plaster, the hollow of the skull first being filled with mud (see Plate 26B). In the best of them the modelling is astonishingly delicate, and shows close observation of anatomical structure; again the eyes are of inlaid shell.

The presence of arrowheads shows that the bow and arrow had been invented, while sickle blades give the first indications of agriculture. Man was no longer content to be entirely dependent on the caprices of nature for his safety and food supply. Settlements of this period are found in parts which are now desert, as at Wadi Dhobai east of Zizia, and typical implements can be found all over the country.

13

The greatest discovery of the Neolithic period was, perhaps, the method of making pottery. This seems to have occurred about 5000 B.C., and must have revolutionized living conditions just as much as the original discovery of flint knapping or flaking. From this time on archaeologists trace the evolution and spread of culture more by the remains of pottery than by any other means. For pottery is fragile but easy to produce, and once broken is thrown away. Each race evolved its own styles and forms, the fashions of which changed with the periods. So it is at once the most abundant and the most distinctive product of any people, and the trained archaeologist can with considerable assurance and accuracy assign a place and date to even quite small fragments. There is some indication that the dolmens—which are boxlike structures made of a flat slab or slabs of stone laid upon a rough wall of smaller slabs set upright—may be the burial places of this period, though some authorities consider them to belong to the succeeding, Chalcolithic, culture. There are fields of dolmens to be seen in many parts of northern Jordan, notably in the Jordan valley in the foothills to the east of Damiah bridge, in the foothills east of Talailat Ghassul, and in the hill country near Hasban, east of Jarash, and around Irbid. To this period probably belong also the many stone circles which are found here and there, sometimes in close relation to the dolmens.

Chalcolithic, 4500–3000 B.C.

The tempo of development speeded up considerably, and hardly had pottery been evolved when an even more epoch-making technique was discovered—the smelting of copper. But early efforts were tentative, and flint implements continued to be used for some time in this period, which was one of experiment in metallurgy.

The excavations at Talailat Ghassul in the Jordan valley give us a picture of life in this age, probably about 3500 B.C. Here was a village of some size, with well-built houses, some made of sun-dried bricks on a rough stone foundation, some made entirely of mud bricks. The roofs were probably of wood, reeds, and mud, as are those of many houses in the valley today. The walls of some houses were plastered and painted in bright colors with representations of men, stars, and other, sometimes geometrical, motifs. Pottery was very advanced (Plate 2A), being well fired, and there were many varieties of shape and decoration, the latter often consisting of elaborate geometric designs painted in red or brown. On the bases of some of the pots are imprints of woven and coiled basketwork, the mat on which the vase was made, while pierced circular stones suggest spindle whorls and weaving. Women decorated themselves with beads of shell and stone, and men, if the paintings are interpreted correctly, were bearded and tattooed; one figure seems to wear a pair of embroidered slippers.

Altogether this and the period immediately following, called the Early Bronze Age, can be considered prosperous and progressive, and there must have been security in the country for settlements were not strongly fortified.

THE BRONZE AGE

Early Bronze, 3000–2100 B.C.

This period is a direct continuation and development of the Chalcolithic, with metal being used in greater quantities, and such objects as swords, daggers and large spearheads being made of copper. Incidentally, the title Bronze Age is somewhat of a misnomer for the Early and Middle periods, as all implements that have so far been analyzed have turned out to be copper and not bronze. The name was acquired in the early days of archaeology, and, like many wrong names, has stuck.

No sites of this period have as yet been excavated in East Jordan, though pockets of occupational debris were found on bedrock in the excavation at Dhiban. But there is ample evidence for their existence in the remains of pottery which can be seen scattered on the surface of some tells and from large groups of pottery and other objects found in rock-cut tombs in various parts of the country. Settlements are thickest in the north, but a thin line of them stretches from north to south, from the Yarmuk to Shobak, south of which no remains of the period have yet been found. This may indicate the line of the trade route, which

15

from the southernmost point turned off to Palestine and Egypt, or may represent the limit of the land which was, under the then-existing methods of agriculture, capable of maintaining a settled population.

Middle Bronze, 2100–1500 B.C.

The Early Bronze Age was brought to an end by an invasion of nomads, who, while their culture was much inferior to that of the Early Bronze people, were apparently more warlike, for they captured and destroyed all the principal towns and villages and interrupted the steady cultural growth that had been going on. But it was only a temporary halt, for the nomads were themselves driven out by a northern invader, the Hyksos or Shepherd kings of the Bible. These people brought with them a vastly superior culture, and as the country was, presumably, in confusion, they had no difficulty in establishing themselves and spreading their power as far as Egypt, which they conquered and ruled for some time. An entirely new type of pottery appears, very highly developed both in technique and beauty of form (Plate 2B), and the shapes and styles which had a steady development throughout the Chalcolithic and Early Bronze periods soon cease to exist. Luxury goods start to appear, imported largely from Egypt, and one gets the impression of a much wider and freer cultural life springing up.

Another significant change, however, is that strongly fortified towns and villages now appear; the period of internal security is gone and is not really recovered until Roman times. The Hyksos, too, introduced the horse and chariot into the Middle East.

So far as East Jordan is concerned, there is at present little evidence that the Hyksos culture had much effect there; the characteristic pottery and other objects have so far been found only in tombs at Amman, Naur and Mount Nebo. In fact, it is difficult to know just what was happening at this time in the rest of the country. It is possible, of course, that the Hyksos did not try to conquer it—there was not much in the way of spoils for them there—and it remained under the control of the nomads already referred to, but there is more to the problem than that.

The Hyksos were driven out by the Egyptians about 1500 B.C., and the founding of the great Egyptian empire of the eighteenth dynasty ushers in the next period.

Late Bronze, 1500–1200 B.C.

To return to the problem of the occupation of East Jordan during this period: on the basis of a surface examination of hundreds of sites up and down the length and breadth of East Jordan, the theory has been propounded that the country was unoccupied from about 1900 to about 1300 B.C.—that is, a period of some 600 years, during part of the Middle and practically the whole of the Late Bronze Ages. It is suggested that a nomadic population only was present at this time.

It has already been shown, however, that, at least as far as the district of Ammon is concerned, there was a sedentary population during the Hyksos phase of the Middle Bronze, for large family tombs well equipped with burial objects, such as those found at Amman and Naur, are not the work of nomads. Further evidence has recently come to light in the form of a small temple which was discovered when the new aerodrome at Amman was being built. It contained great quantities of pottery and other objects, including much imported Mycenaean and Cypriot pottery and Egyptian stone vases, which are typical of the period 1600 to 1300 B.C. This also implies an urban population in Amman, for a temple requires worshippers and a priesthood. Further, at Madaba a large tomb was found which dates from the end of the Late Bronze to the Early Iron periods.

At the time the survey referred to was made we had no groups of local pottery dated in the Middle and Late Bronze Ages, and it was the absence of imported wares so common in Palestine at that time that suggested an unoccupied country. From the recently found and well-dated groups we see that the local pottery of the period is slightly different from that of contemporary Palestine, so maybe the sherds found during the survey should be re-examined in the light of these finds. At least we know that Ammon was flourishing then, for the temple, though small, was a rich one.

From the Middle Bronze Age onward the outline as shown by archaeology can be amplified by the Biblical stories, and we must retrace our steps a little to complete the picture.

According to the accounts in Genesis, the southern part of the country from the Wadi Hasa to the Gulf of Aqaba was called Seir—modern Shara, which is the same word—and was inhabited by Horites or cave dwellers. This district was also called Edom, and given to Esau, whose descendants gradually ousted or exterminated the Horites and occupied the whole land. Lists are given of the sons of Seir the Horite and of Esau, who are called "dukes," more properly sheikhs, and the kings of Edom and their capital towns are mentioned. Only one of these towns can now be identified, Bozrah, the modern Busairah near Tafilah. Also a battle with Midian, the southern neighbor of Edom, "in the field of Moab," is recorded. This account, perhaps about 2000 B.C., shows us people living in the tribal style, each tribe with its own sheikhs, and a "sheikh of sheikhs" or king, whose decision was final in all administrative matters and who led the army in the day of battle.

Mention of Midian and Moab, southern and northern neighbors respectively, shows that these kingdoms were also then in existence, and the traditional origin of Moab and its northern neighbor Ammon is told in the story of Lot and his daughters. These two states, with a common origin, seem also to have had common interests, and one is often confused with the other in later Biblical stories. But their boundaries are clearly stated, Moab from the Wadi Hasa (Zered) to the Mojib (Arnon), and Ammon from the Mojib to the Zarka (Jabbok). In early days, however, it is stated that Moab and Ammon are occupied by races of giants, called Emim in the former and Rephaim and Zuzim in the latter place. A punitive expedition of Chedorlaomer king of Elam broke up the power of these giants, and of the "Horites in their Mount Seir," and probably made the occupation of the country by Esau, Moab and the Beni Ammi much easier.

There is no further Biblical reference to events in East Jordan until the Exodus. The date of this event has been placed by scholars either in the fifteenth or the fourteenth century B.C., but the bulk of evidence seems to be in favor of the later date, perhaps about 1320 B.C. It is curious that archaeology suggests an unoccupied country and that the Bible should be silent on Jordan in this period, but whichever date for the Exodus is the right one, the story requires a fully occupied Edom, Moab and Ammon, and this cannot happen in a generation.

Numbers XX

When the children of Israel arrived at Kadesh, in south Palestine, they found Edom a fully organized state with a king at its head. To him they wrote from Kadesh, "a city in the uttermost of thy borders," for permission to pass through Edom peacefully, "along the king's highway, not turning aside to the right hand nor to the left." They were refused, and told they would be attacked if they tried to pass. A second appeal produced a show of force on the part of the king which persuaded the Israelites that he meant what he said. The reference to the "king's highway" is interesting and confirms the suggestion of a caravan or trade route running north and south through the country. The Israelites were thus forced to go around the borders of Edom, which they did by going down to the Gulf of Aqaba and then apparently turning northeast towards Maan. From there they continued north, almost along the line of the present desert road, past Wadi Hasa (Zered) and the Mojib (Arnon), which was the beginning of the Amorite country, for it would seem that these people had meantime ousted Ammon from the vicinity. Sihon was then the Amorite king, with his capital at Heshbon near Madaba, and to him the Israelites applied for permission to pass through his land. He refused and gave battle to them, but was defeated and his land occupied "from Arnon to Jabbok, even unto the children of Ammon."

In another version of the same story, Moses, in asking permission to pass peacefully and be allowed to buy food and water, adds, "as the children of Esau which dwell in Seir and the Moabites which dwell in Ar," implying that his treatment there was favorable. Such strange inconsistencies, of which there are many, make the compilation of a history of the period somewhat difficult. This same second account also says that the Israelites killed every man, woman and child in the towns which were so unfortunate as to be captured by them. Some time previous to this, Sihon had been at war with Moab, and had destroyed the town of Ar (perhaps modern Rabbah or Karak), and the "lords of the high places of Arnon," meaning the images of the gods in the various sanctuaries. The chief deity of Moab was called Chemosh, who is later said to be also the god of Ammonites, but the quotation shows that each locality had its own Baal or Lord, who would merely be a variant of the chief deity. Other towns mentioned in the narrative are Dibon and Madaba, both well known today, and Nophah, unidentified so far.

Numbers XXII–XXIII

Although they defeated Sihon, there were apparently other strong forces to the west, for the Israelites were unable to break through to the Jordan valley, as a short cut to Palestine, but had to make a detour north to Bashan and Edrei (modern Deraa). After defeating Og king of Bashan (whose "iron bedstead" was then in Amman) they were able to pass down to the Jordan valley, and encamped in the "plains of Moab," probably in the vicinity of modern Shunat Nimrin. The king of Moab was then Balak son of Zippor, and being extremely worried and "distressed" at the presence of the victorious Israelites on his border he proceeded to form an alliance with the five kings of Midian, which was the country to the southeast of Aqaba, modern Hijaz. Together they invited Balaam, apparently a famous prophet and seer, to come and curse the children of Israel before they made war on them, but two deputations had to be sent before he would agree to come, and then only on the clear understanding that he could say nothing except what God told him to say.

The subsequent account gives an interesting glimpse of some of the religious ceremonies of the time. Balak took Balaam up to the high places of Baal, and was ordered by him to build seven altars and sacrifice a bull and a ram on each. Having done this,

Balaam told Balak to stand by his burnt offering while he went off to a "bare height" and received word from God. Returning, he found Balak and all the princes of Moab waiting by the sacrifices, and he then proceeded to bless Israel instead of cursing them as was expected. Balak must have been taken aback, but was not daunted, and suggested that at a different spot Balaam might get different ideas. Accordingly the sacrifices and ceremonial were repeated on top of Pisgah, but with precisely the same results. Still Balak did not despair, and repeated the process at a third spot, again with the same results. After this Balak gave it up, and also apparently abandoned the idea of fighting the Israelites, who for some reason turned their attention to the assembled Midianites. There was a battle, in the course of which Balaam himself was killed, seemingly fighting against the people he had so recently blessed and for whom he had prophesied a great future.

The Israelite tribes of Gad and Reuben and half Manasseh settled themselves into the conquered territory of the Ammonites, Amorites and Bashan, and built, or perhaps rebuilt, many towns and villages, a few of which can still be identified. Moses went or was taken to the top of Mount Nebo, which was a Moabite sanctuary, and surveyed the Promised Land. There he died and was buried opposite the sanctuary of Baal at Peor—a strange end for one who had all his life been fighting against those very deities. Soon after the Israelites under Joshua passed over the Jordan, and East Jordan settled down to a long period of bitter quarrels and fights with them.

It is usual to divide this age into three periods, Iron I, Iron II and Iron III, beginning about 1200 B.C. and ending in 330 B.C.; but, as there is almost complete continuity during the period, for purposes of this brief survey the sub-divisions have been omitted.

Archaeology gives us a few highly interesting but very brief glimpses of conditions at the beginning of this period. At Balua, a small ruined village on the Moabite side of the Arnon not far from Rabbah, was found a stele, a large rough-shaped block of black basalt, on which was carved an inscription of four lines and three human figures (Plate 3B). The figures apparently represent two gods and a king between them, and everything about them shows very strong Egyptian influence, though the work is certainly not Egyptian. The deities both wear Egyptian crowns and one carries an Egyptian "Uas" scepter, and they and the king wear Egyptian dress. The only un-Egyptian features are the king's headdress and the moon and sun (?) symbols above his shoulders. Unfortunately the inscription is badly weathered, and not even the alphabet used can be definitely determined. It is considered by some authorities that this was originally an Early Bronze Age stele re-used in the early Iron Age.

The tomb at Madaba, previously referred to, shows us the kinds of things people were using and wearing during the end of the Late Bronze Age and the beginning of the Iron Age. The pottery is of extraordinarily poor quality, perhaps the poorest in the long history of ceramics in Jordan, being badly made and fired and the forms clumsy. There are bronze daggers, one with a handle originally inlaid in wood, bronze arrow-heads and some pieces of bronze scale armor. For ornament there are bronze and iron bracelets, anklets, earrings and finger rings, toggle pins for fastening the clothes, also beads of stone and glazed paste. A few scarabs, typical of the Egyptian nineteenth and twentieth dynasties, and a glazed Egyptian eye amulet complete the picture (Plate 4).

Such strong Egyptian influence as is shown by these two finds is not suggested in any of the Biblical narratives, but Egyptian records themselves make mention of places in East Jordan in the nineteenth dynasty.

Judges III

Returning to the Biblical account, in the book of Judges we find Eglon king of Moab raiding and even settling in Palestine. At Jericho, about 1150 B.C. the Israelites, in alliance with Ammon, and the Amalekites who came from southern Palestine, after killing Eglon by a trick, drove the Moabites out of the country "with very great slaughter."

Judges VI

Next we read of the Midianites attacking Israel. As their territory was to the southeast, beyond Aqaba they must have passed through or been in alliance with East Jordan before they could attack Palestine. Particular mention of their camels shows that there were nomad forces with them. Gideon, then judge of the Israelites, defeated them by a subterfuge, and captured two princes named Oreb and Zeeb. He pursued the fleeing forces over the Jordan, apparently by the Damiah ford, past Succoth in the valley and up the Jabbok to Jogbehah (modern Jubaihah, near Amman). Zebah and Zalmunna, the kings of Midian, fled to Karkur, somewhere in the Wadi Sirhan, on the way back to their country, but Gideon caught up with them and finally defeated them there. The two kings were made prisoner, and he returned by the same route to mete out punishment to the people of Penuel and Succoth for refusing to help him on his outward journey. He then slew the two kings of Midian, and "took the crescents that were on their camels' necks." Considerable spoil was also taken, chiefly of gold earrings which the men of Midian wore "because they were Ishmaelites."

Judges X

Soon after the Ammonites were raiding first those of the Israelites settled in their country, and then, finding success there, farther afield into Palestine. Jephthah was now leader of Israel, and the king of Ammon sent to him to demand the restoration of such of their territory as had been taken away by Moses. The request was, of course, refused, and in the battle which followed the Ammonites were driven out and the Israelites even raided into the country around Heshbon. In the beginning of Saul's reign the Ammonites were again raiding the Israelites at Jabesh Gilead, and were again defeated by a trick. Nahash was then king of Ammon.

I Samuel

During all this time there had been little mention of Edom or Moab. David frequently took refuge in the Wadi Arabah, Edom,

Moab and perhaps Ammon when he was in hiding from Saul; and when he became king, about 1000 B.C., he attacked both Moab and Edom and subdued them, in spite of family ties and the fact that they had frequently given him sanctuary. In Moab he slew two-thirds of the population. The Edomites had been raiding in southern Palestine, and were defeated there by a force under Joab, who pursued them back to their own country and proceeded to slaughter every male he could lay hands on. A young Edomite prince, Hadad, escaped to Egypt where he was well received by the reigning Pharaoh Siamon or perhaps Pasebkhanu, and was granted a house and estate and married the queen's sister.

II Samuel X

David sent a deputation to Hanun king of Ammon to console him on the death of his father Nahash, about 995 B.C. Nahash had apparently done David some good turn, probably giving him refuge, and David wished to requite this. The deputation was, however, received with suspicion and publicly insulted. This, of course, led to a war, in which the Ammonites were aided by a Syrian confederacy, but were defeated and driven back into their city, Rabbath Ammon, modern Amman. A siege followed and as the Israelites succeeded in taking the water supply, the city was forced to capitulate (see pages 48–49). Apparently Hanun's brother Shobi was appointed in his place and became tributary to David, for when the latter in his fight with Absalom crossed the Jordan, Shobi and other Jordan sheikhs brought supplies to him.

II Kings

David's hold on the country was never very strong, and on his death, about 960 B.C., Edom at least regained a large measure of independence. The prince Hadad returned from Egypt and ruled over his country again, and Solomon seems to have retained only the port of Ezion Geber near Aqaba. But he made alliances with the country by taking wives from Edom, Moab and Ammon; from the latter place he took a daughter of Hanun.

Here again archaeology enables us to amplify the Biblical account. Excavation on the probable site of Ezion Geber (Tell al Khalaifah) shows that its chief industry was the smelting of copper, which was obtained from the mines in the Wadi Arabah. The town was roughly rectangular in plan, enclosed in a thick wall with an imposing gateway, and the furnaces and kilns were on the north side of the town. These show a very high degree of skill in their layout, and the site chosen is at a point where the wind blowing from the north down the Wadi Arabah is at its strongest, so that considerable temperatures could be generated. Earthenware crucibles with a capacity of 13 cubic feet were also found. Mud brick was used in all the buildings, and pottery types show curious differences from those found in other parts of the country. The explanation of this may be that there were strong connections with South Arabia through trading, and the inhabitants must have been a fairly cosmopolitan lot. The best-laid-out town was the earliest, of about the time of Solomon; there were five occupation levels on the site.

In other parts of East Jordan a surface examination of hundreds of ancient sites shows that despite the wars, raids and slaughtering recorded in the Old Testament, the level of prosperity and culture was steadily rising. Fortresses, strongly built of big flinty blocks, were constructed along the borders and at strategic points, and the great number of small village sites which exist suggests a largely agricultural population.

Upon the death of Solomon, about 931 B.C., his kingdom split up into two states, Judah and Israel, which were continually at war with each other and within themselves. Biblical accounts of the period are confused and contradictory, and it is difficult to unravel a consecutive history. Jehoshaphat, king of Judah, built a fleet at Ezion Geber which was destroyed by a storm before it could ever set sail. There is also a statement that "there was no king in Edom, a deputy was king." Also during Jehoshaphat's reign there is a muddled account of an attack on Judah by Moab and Ammon in alliance with Edom. The battle apparently ended by the Ammonites and Moabites attacking and killing all the Edomites and then slaughtering each other while Jehoshaphat and his people looked on and, when the last person had been slain, rushed in and stripped the bodies of their valuables, a task which took them three days.

The Moabite Stone (compare II Kings III)

From this period, however, we have the only contemporary historical record so far found in the country. It is a large stele inscribed and set up by Mesha king of Moab in his capital Dhiban, and records his battles with the kings of Israel (Plate 3A). The following is a complete translation of his unique record:

I (am) Mesha, son of Chemosh—[. . .], king of Moab, the Dibonite— my father (had) reigned over Moab thirty years, and I reigned after my father,—(who) made this high place for Chemosh in Qarhoh [. . .] because he saved me from all the kings and caused me to triumph over all my adversaries. As for Omri, king of Israel, he humbled Moab many years (lit. days), for Chemosh was angry at his land. And his son followed him and he also said, "I will humble Moab." In my time he spoke (thus), but I have triumphed over him and over his house, while Israel hath perished for ever! (Now) Omri had occupied the land of Medeba, and (Israel) had dwelt there in his time and half the time of his son (Ahab), forty years, but Chemosh dwelt there in my time.

And I built Baal-meon, making a reservoir in it, and I built Qaryaten. Now the men of Gad had always dwelt in the land of Ataroth, and the king of Israel had built Ataroth for them; but I fought against the town and took it and slew all the people of the town as satiation (intoxication) for Chemosh and Moab. And I brought back from there Arel (or Oriel), its chieftain, dragging him before Chemosh in Kerioth, and I settled there men of Sharon and men of Maharith. And Chemosh said to me, "Go, take Nebo from Israel!" So I went by night and fought against it from the break of dawn until noon, taking it and slaying all, seven thousand men, boys, women, girls and maid-servants, for I had devoted them to destruction for (the god) Ashtar-Chemosh. And I took from there the [. . .] of Yahweh, dragging them before Chemosh. And the king of Israel had built Jahaz, and he dwelt there while he was fighting against me, but Chemosh drove him out before me. And I took from Moab two hundred men, all first class (warriors), and set them against Jahaz and took it in order to attach it to (the district of) Dibon.

It was I (who) built Qarhoh, the wall of *the forests* and the wall of the citadel; I also built its gates and I built its towers and I built the

26

king's house, and I made both of its reservoirs for water inside the town. And there was no cistern inside the town at Qarhoh, so I said to all the people, "Let each of you make a cistern for himself in his house!" And I cut *beams* for Qarhoh with Israelite captives. I built Aroer, and I made the highway in the Arnon (valley); I built Beth-bamoth, for it had been destroyed; I built Bezer—for it lay in ruins—with fifty men of Dibon, for all Dibon is (my) loyal dependency.

And I reigned [*in peace*] *over* the hundred towns which I had added to the land. And I built [. . .] Medeba and Beth-diblathen and Beth-baal-meon, and I set there the [. . .] of the land. And as for Hauronen, there dwelt in it [. . . And] Chemosh said to me, "Go down, fight against Hauronen. And I went down [and I fought against the town and I took it], and Chemosh dwelt there in my time. . . .

The son of Omri king of Israel was Ahab, who was contemporary with Jehoshaphat of Judah. In the Biblical account Mesha is called a sheepmaster, who pays heavy tribute to Israel, and his revolt is placed in the reign of Jehoram son of Ahab. This is about 850 B.C. Israel, Judah and Edom allied together to recover Moab, and set out to attack Mesha from the south by way of Edom, which again had a king of its own. They achieved some success, and besieged Mesha in Karak; "Then he took his eldest son that should have reigned in his stead, and offered him for a burnt offering upon the wall. And there was great indignation against Israel; and they departed from him, and returned to their own land." It is difficult to see why this act of Mesha's should have had the effects it did, but it may have had some implication which we do not now understand. Mesha had clearly extended his kingdom north of the Arnon and occupied at least the southern part of the Ammonite kingdom, for many of the towns mentioned in the stele, such as Madaba, are north of his capital, Dhiban, which is itself north of the Arnon.

In the reign of the next king of Judah, Jehoram, Edom also revolted, and threw off the Hebrew yoke: a later king, Amaziah, beat off an Edomite attack on south Palestine, and pursued the attackers back to their own country. He even captured Sela, or Petra, the capital, and from its high cliffs hurled 10,000 prisoners to their death (see page 103). Ezion Geber, now renamed Elath, remained in Judaean hands for some time, and a fine seal of the king Jotham, grandson of Amaziah, was found in the excavations there.

The discovery of two complete statues and remains of two others outside the north end of the Amman citadel has added considerably to our knowledge of the culture of this period (Plate 6B). The style, dress and other details of the figures reflect influences from all the great civilizations around, Phoenician, Egyptian and Assyrian, which indeed is what one would expect from the geographical position of the country. These statues are unique in being the only full, free-standing figures in the round of this early period, and presumably of indigenous workmanship, yet discovered in Jordan or Palestine. There is a short inscription of two lines on the plinth of one of the figures, the script being similar to that of the Mesha stele, but it is unfortunately badly rubbed and difficult to interpret. They probably date from about 800 B.C.

The Assyrian Annals

The power of Assyria now began to rise on the horizon of Near Eastern history, which by its force and brutality made a profound impression on the peoples of Syria, Palestine and Jordan. About 800 B.C. Adad Nirari made the first of a series of attacks on those countries, and for a time overran East Jordan as far as Edom, which is separately mentioned in the Assyrian records. During the next few years the country seems to have been in a state of upheaval, the Assyrian domination was thrown off and Elath was recaptured by the Edomites. In 738 Tiglath Pileser III overran the whole country, and the king of Ammon, Sanibu, with Chemosh Nadab, king of Moab, and Shalman of Edom had to pay tribute and submit to being controlled by governors.

An attempted revolt against Assyria by Palestine when Sennacherib became king in 705 was not supported in Jordan, where Pudiel was king of Ammon, another Chemosh Nadab in Moab and Airammu in Edom. The revolt was soon subdued, and the East Jordan states allowed to retain a nominal independence.

Under Esarhaddon, son of Sennacherib, about 680 B.C., the kings were still paying tribute. A letter to the Assyrian king reports, among other things, that the royal governors have brought two mannas of gold from Pudiel of Ammon, one manna of gold from Musuri of Moab, about twelve mannas of silver from Qaus-gabr of Edom, whose name has also been found on seal impressions at Tell al Khalaifah, or Elath. This is the earliest record of Qaus as the name of an Edomite deity; it occurs frequently in later periods. Ashur-bani-pal, the successor of Esarhaddon, continued a policy of expansion, but while his attention was taken up with Egypt a serious revolt of the Bedu in the Wadi Sirhan broke out. Under their leader Yatha they attacked Jordan and extended their activities as far north as Homs in Syria. Ammuladi, king of the Kedar Arabs, was captured by Chemosh Khaltay king of Moab during a raid on that country. Amminadab was king of Ammon, and we have some interesting contemporary objects from Amman bearing his name.

About sixty years ago a seal of "Adoni-pelet, servant of AmmiNadab," was found in Amman, and more recently a rock-cut tomb on the Citadel slopes has yielded a splendid group of pottery and other objects, including a seal in a silver mount of "Adoni-nur, servant of AmmiNadab" (Plate 4). The title "servant" evidently implies some high court official, and the first seal may also have come from this tomb, two brothers, or perhaps father and son, succeeding each other in the post. There are several other fine seals in the group, one bearing the name Shub-El, and all showing the dominating Assyrian influence in their style. Three large pottery coffins are an unusual feature in the group, and other objects include silver finger rings and earrings and a very fine small gold fibula. Another tomb of approximately the same period was found on a hilltop to the south of the opposite side of the valley from the Adoni-nur tomb. This contained the usual group of pottery, an interesting model of a horse and rider, the latter's head unfortunately missing, which shows in careful detail the type of harness used, including a tassel hanging down the horse's forehead such as is still seen today; also an ivory seal bearing the name Allat-tesha, which suggests that Allat was already one of the goddesses worshipped in Ammon; her cult was common in later times.

Yet a third tomb of the period was found at Muqabalain, just southwest of Amman, in which were a chalcedony seal and a cylinder seal, both of Assyrian type, but there were also imports from the west in the form of two fine multi-colored glass perfume flasks. Again there are pottery horses and riders, this time complete, and the rider wears a high, pointed hat.

In this period the Assyrian records make the first historical reference to the Nabataeans, later so prominent in Jordan history, who at this time occupied the country south and east of Edom, the old land of Midian.

The Rise of Babylon

The Assyrian empire ended with the fall of Nineveh in 612 B.C., and the Babylonian began to rise in its place. Revolts broke out everywhere in the absence of firm control, and during the reign of Nebuchadnezzar, the Moabites and Ammonites were raiding in Palestine, where Jehoiakim was king of Judah. Soon after, there seems to have been an attempt to form an alliance of Jordan, Palestine and part of Syria to defy Nebuchadnezzar, but the Babylonian king took instant action and nothing came of it except the carrying off of the Jews into captivity. Many of them had, however, fled to Moab and Edom for safety, and when Gedaliah was set up as governor of Judah under Babylon they started to collect around him again. For some reason not clear, Baalis king of Ammon hired a certain Ishmael to kill Gedaliah, which was successfully accomplished.

Little is known of the history of East Jordan in the next few decades, but it seems that about 580 B.C. the Nabataeans were beginning to occupy Edom, and the Edomites were being forced out into south Palestine. The whole Near East was at this time in a state of flux; the old kingdoms, Egypt, Syria and Mesopotamia, were falling to pieces, and the new Persian and Greek kingdoms were coming into being. The remaining Jews were practically driven out of Palestine and other peoples were filtering in.

The Persian Empire, 549–331 B.C.

Under the Persians, Jordan and Palestine were placed under the Arabian satrapy or governorship. About 500 B.C. the Persians allowed some of the Jews who had been carried into captivity to return to Palestine. The Edomites were by now firmly settled in south Palestine, later known as Idumea, and the Moabites and Ammonites frequently attacked the Jews with the object of preventing them from rebuilding the temple in Jerusalem, which was the outward and visible sign of their resettlement in the land. Ammon and Moab also were fighting among themselves, and Ammon recovered the country as far as the Arnon. In this period a certain Tobias, of Jewish extraction, seems to have been ruler in Ammon, and was founder of a dynasty which controlled that country for some centuries, for the Tobiads are mentioned again in Ptolemaic times. He was one of the chief opponents of the rebuilding of the temple.

THE HELLENISTIC PERIOD, 331–63 B.C.

Nothing more is known of events here until the time of Alexander's conquests in 333 B.C. When he died, Egypt, Palestine, Jordan and southern Syria came under the control of his general Ptolemy, who made his center in Egypt. The Nabataeans by this time were well established in Edom with their capital at Petra (see pages 103 *ff.*). Stories of their wealth caused Antigonus of Syria to send an army against them, about 311 B.C., but after having seized the capital and removed all possible booty, carelessness in setting out his camp enabled the Nabataeans to attack and annihilate the Greeks. At a second attempt, all the Nabataeans withdrew from Petra, leaving only a few old men there, who bought off the general Demetrius and so secured the peace of the district.

The northern part of Syria fell to the lot of Seleucus, another of Ptolemy's generals, but he was not content with his share and, without much opposition, took over Jordan. Ptolemy II, about 284 B.C., set out to remedy this situation, and invaded and captured Ammon and part of Midian, though he seems to have left the Nabataeans alone. The Greek culture was received with great acclaim in the Near East, and new towns which now began to spring up in Jordan, and old ones which were being rebuilt, all contained elements of Greek art and architecture. It influenced even the remote Nabataeans and brought about a marked change in their architecture. Coins also began to make their appearance, modelled on the Greek styles. Many cities were renamed in honor of their Greek rebuilders, such as Amman, which became Philadelphia, and Jarash, which became Antioch.

General prosperity and culture started on an upward trend, which only really ceased with the Arab invasion in the seventh century A.D. International relations were considerably facilitated by the adoption of Greek as the language and writing of culture through the Near East.

Hostilities between the Ptolemies of Egypt and the Seleucids of Syria enabled the Nabataeans to extend their kingdom to the north. They supported the Syrians against the Egyptians, and in a treaty made in 197 B.C. Antiochus III of Syria retained Palestine, Syria and Jordan. During his reign, one Hyrcanus, a Jew from Palestine and probably a member of the Tobiad family, established for himself a small state in Ammon, with its center at the present Araq al Amir west of Amman. He controlled the neighborhood for about twelve years, until finally Antiochus IV had to send an expedition against him. Realizing the futility of resistance, Hyrcanus committed suicide in 175 B.C. The edicts of Antiochus IV against the Jews caused a rebellion which was led by Judas Maccabeus, who in three successive years, 167 to 165 B.C., defeated four armies sent against him by Antiochus, and established a Jewish state. On the death of Antiochus in 164 B.C., Judas started to enlarge his state by invading Ammon. The Ammonites under a leader named Timotheus were defeated, but escaped to make trouble in Gilead. Judas again defeated them at Ashtoreth Karnaim, and Timotheus was killed there.

Another Syrian army was sent in 163 B.C., which defeated the Jews, but did not complete the work, and yet another had to be sent in 161 B.C. This time the Jews were finally beaten, and many who had taken refuge in Arbila (probably Irbid) were massacred.

Less than a century later, in 84 B.C., they were again up in arms, with even more success, and Alexander Jannaeus, who led their forces, at his death controlled the whole of Jordan to the Wadi Hasa. Only the Nabataeans remained independent, and they had succeeded in extending their dominion as far as Damascus, maintaining their control over this area until A.D. 106. The first Nabataean king to rule this extended kingdom was Aretas III Philhellen, 95–50 B.C. They do not, however, seem to have exercised direct control over the western part of Jordan which lies between the Mojib and the Yarmuk, though building blocks found at Jarash carved in the form of the Nabataean crowstep pattern, and a bilingual inscription in Nabataean and Greek also found there, show that their influence at least penetrated as far west as that. The recent discovery in a tomb in Amman of two decorated Nabataean bowls confirms this.

ROME AND BYZANTIUM, 63 B.C.–A.D. 636

Meanwhile the new power of Rome had been steadily growing, and the expansion of the empire made it necessary to impose order in Syria and Palestine. This was achieved by Pompey, about 64 B.C., and in East Jordan he restored all the Greek cities which had been destroyed by the Jews and laid the foundations for the commercial league known as the Decapolis. This league originally consisted of Scythopolis (Beisan), Pella (Tabaqat Fahil), Hippos (Fiq); Damascus, Dion (unidentified), Kanatha (Kanawat), Jarash and Philadelphia (Amman). Later other cities were added, notably Arbila (Irbid), Capitolias (Bait Ras), Edrei (Deraa) and Bosra. The country retained complete independence, merely paying taxes to the imperial treasury. The Nabataeans also bought their continued independence for a lump sum. These conditions did not outlast the person who imposed them, and on Pompey's departure all the old revolts broke out afresh.

During the next quiet period, about 40 B.C., Herod the Great,

33

with Mark Antony's backing, was made king of Judea, which included some control of East Jordan. Trouble between Mark Antony and the Nabataeans led to Herod's attacking and defeating them, and driving them out of the northern part of their kingdom. By the time of Herod's death in 4 B.C., Roman influence was everywhere paramount, and East Jordan was divided into three districts under three different controls. In the north was the Decapolis league, independent as far as internal affairs were concerned, in the center from the Zarka to the Arnon (not including Amman) was Peraea, under the Jewish kinglets of Palestine, and in the south was the independent Nabataean kingdom.

Herod the Great was succeeded by Herod the Tetrarch, who married a daughter of the Nabataean king, Aretas IV. He divorced her for his brother's wife Herodias, which insult caused Aretas to send an army against him and defeat him. It was Herod's scandalous behavior while at Machaerus (modern Mukawir, southwest of Madaba) with Herodias and her daughter Salome that caused John the Baptist to denounce him, resulting in John's imprisonment and death at Machaerus.

Strong Roman rule kept the country quiet for some time, but the Jews could not long remain at peace, and about A.D. 64 the Nabataean king Malchus II sent an army to help the Romans against them. Many Jews took refuge in Machaerus, but the Romans destroyed the place and slaughtered the garrison. Finally in A.D. 106, under the Emperor Trajan, the Nabataean kingdom was also broken up, and Jordan lost its independence but gained a long peace. The whole country with the exception of the Decapolis was attached to a new province called Arabia Petraea, with its capital first at Petra and later at Bosra in Syria. The third legion (Cyrenaica) was posted in the north and the fourth (Martia) in the south of the country. Two great camps built to accommodate the latter, at Lajjun near Karak and Adhruh near Petra, can still be seen. The great road of Trajan from Bosra and Aqaba was begun, and finished under Hadrian, and other side roads were opened up all over the country.

The general level of security and prosperity during the next few centuries was higher than it had ever been, shattered only occasionally by the disgraceful intrigues and murders among the Roman emperors, and a few attempts by petty rulers to assert their independence. During the second and third centuries villages and towns sprang into being all over the country, boasting a degree of elegance and architecture never achieved before or since. Details of history in this period are details of petty events, leaving no permanent effects, though one great power was coming more or less quietly into being—Christianity. With the conversion of the Roman emperor in A.D. 333, it became the paramount religion, and under the Byzantine empire, established in A.D. 395 by the Emperor Theodosius, an enormous number of churches sprang up all over the country.

But control was considerably looser under the Byzantine rule, and ominous cracks began to appear in the administrative structure. Many of these were caused by opposing Christian sects, from the squabbles of which the emperors themselves were by no means immune.

In the late sixth and early seventh centuries the Persians were again active, attacking and occupying some of the eastern provinces, including part at least of East Jordan. The Emperor Heraclius (A.D. 610–641), beat them off, and had just succeeded in establishing some order throughout the empire when the Muslim invasion began.

ISLAM A.D. 636

The first clash between Muslims and Byzantines took place at Motah, near Karak, when the Muslims were driven back and their three great leaders, Zaid ibn Harith, Jaafar ibn abu Talib and AbdAllah ibn Ruaha, were killed. They were buried at Mazar, where their tombs are still to be seen in the great mosque. Another army was soon sent out, and at a fateful battle on the Wadi Yarmuk in A.D. 636, the forces of Byzantium were routed, and the victorious Muslims advanced on to Damascus, where eventually the Umayyad Caliphate established its capital.

Some of these early caliphs, being really Bedu, still hankered

35

after the desert, and built themselves palaces and hunting lodges in the east of Jordan, such as Qasr al Amra (Plate 21), Kharanah (Plate 22) and Tuba (Plate 23). As Jordan lies directly on the route between Damascus and Arabia it continued to be of some importance, but the plots of the Abbasside family, which finally destroyed the Umayyads and Jordan with them, were originally hatched at Humaimah, a little village in the Quairah plain south of Maan.

In the ninth century A.D. the conquering Abbassids transferred the capital to Baghdad, and Jordan began to be forgotten; not being on any particular trade route, or producing any natural wealth, the country was left to fall into decay. But it was still of sufficient importance for the crusaders in the twelfth century to occupy part of it and build castles there, the chief of which were Shobak (Plate 5A) and Karak (Plate 11). After that its prosperity declined still further, and it was a country of small, poor villages, scraping a bare existence among the ruins of past splendor. When it passed into Turkish hands in the fifteenth century, their only concern with it was the guarding of the pilgrim road to Mecca, which was on the line of the modern railway.

So the country remained in obscurity until the First World War, when it flashed into the limelight as the scene of Lawrence's exploits. Most of his remarkable campaigns were carried out up and down the length of East Jordan, and he had headquarters at Aqaba and Azraq (Plate 12A). After the war the country was included, on special terms, in the British mandate for Palestine, and in 1921 the Amir AbdAllah, second son of King Husein of the Hijaz, was invited to become the ruler of Trans-Jordan under the high commissioner for Palestine. A semi-independent form of government was introduced, and the ubiquitous Arab Legion, which every traveller in the country has sooner or later to thank for its assistance, courtesy and hospitality, was organized to maintain law and order. Slow, steady development marked the period between the two wars.

During the last war Jordan again became of potential importance when there was a threat of Egypt being overrun, and Aqaba was hurriedly made into a port for bringing supplies to

36

Syria and the north. The Arab Legion acquitted itself nobly during the Iraqi revolt and the Syrian campaign, but fortunately the war came no nearer than that.

In 1946 the country was granted complete independence, and the Amir AbdAllah became the first king of the Hashemite Kingdom of Trans-Jordan. The tempo of development began to increase considerably, but the giving up of the Palestine mandate by Great Britain in 1948 and the subsequent fighting between Jew and Arab momentarily checked this. The enormous influx of refugees imposed a severe strain on the country's resources; some idea of the difficulties to be faced can be gained from the fact that in May 1948 the population of Amman doubled in two weeks. The government administration was, however, sufficiently well founded to withstand the impact, and about half a million refugees were absorbed in the country and cared for without undue hardship to them. Various forms of relief were later provided by the United Nations and other organizations. Jordan was almost the only country to welcome the refugees and give them full scope to work and carry on their trades and professions—not without detriment to the indigenous Jordanian population.

In 1951 that part of Palestine still in Arab hands was united with Trans-Jordan to become the Hashemite Kingdom of Jordan.

Chapter III

IRBID · UMM QAIS · BAIT RAS · TELL AL ASHIAR ·
TELL AL HUSN · QALAT AL RABADH · AJLUN · HIS-
TORY AND MONUMENTS OF AMMAN · ARAQ AL AMIR ·
MADABA · MOUNT NEBO · ZARKA MAIN

PRIOR to the termination of the mandate in 1948 the city
and district of Irbid lay athwart one of the main routes from
Jordan to the port of Haifa via Tiberias and Nazareth, and
was consequently an important center of transit trade. But despite the loss of this advantage, the city has continued to flourish
and grow considerably, and is now second only to Amman in
size and population, for it is the administrative center of one of
the most fertile districts in the country. Nearly all its expansion
has taken place since the end of the last war, the chief deterrent
previously being the absence of any natural water supply in the
immediate vicinity of the town and lack of funds to install any
system of bringing a supply from a distance. Water is now
pumped in from a spring some 11 miles to the northeast.

IRBID

The city is partly built over a large artificial mound, which
conceals the remains of the earliest Irbid, that of the Early Bronze
Age about 2500 B.C. This ancient town was surrounded by a
great wall built of huge blocks of basalt, a part of which is still
exposed on the western side of the mound. A fine stretch of this
same wall could previously be seen on the east of the Tell, bor-
dering the main street there, but this was torn down by the

municipality in 1937 during a road-widening project. There is no archaeological evidence for occupation of the site between the Early–Middle Bronze Ages and Roman times; the reason may well be that some natural catastrophe, such as an earthquake, caused the drying up of the water supply, a difficulty which only the engineering genius of the Romans could overcome. They brought water in a conduit from somewhere near Remthe not only to Irbid but also to Gadara (Umm Qais).

Fig. 2. Map II showing the district in the region of Amman and Irbid

Irbid is generally identified with Arbila, a city of the Decapolis, and in earlier times there were many signs in the form of architectural remains and inscriptions that it had been a place of considerable importance and size in Roman and Byzantine times.

39

But the rapid growth of the modern town has effectively effaced such traces, and nothing remains but a few carved stones and inscribed fragments. The present city is of no particular interest or architectural merit, and the use of basalt as a building stone certainly adds no touch of beauty to the scene.

UMM QAIS

From Irbid a track leads northwest to Umm Qais, passing through Bait Ras; the former is identified with Gadara, scene of the miracle of the Gadarene swine, and the latter with Capitolias, another city of the Decapolis.

Gadara was a Graeco-Roman town of considerable pretentions, even boasting a university which produced the great poet Meleager and some other writers famous in their day. All that now remains of its glory are two small theaters, built of basalt, and a large area of tumbled stones and column drums, and some rock-cut tombs. It is by no means clear why it is in such ruins, as for the last 1,000 years there has been no town or village nearby to use it as a stone quarry, and it is, further, on an almost isolated spur of land, with steep slopes on all sides but the east. The best thing about Umm Qais is the magnificent view across the Sea of Galilee to the north and down the Jordan valley to the south.

In the bed of Yarmuk gorge, just north of Umm Qais, lie the hot springs of Hammah, and a rough track, passable to cars, leads down to them. In the season, a number of visitors make the rather bumpy journey there in order to take the waters.

BAIT RAS

Bait Ras, nearer to Irbid, is even more ruinous than Gadara, and the modern village sprawls its poverty over most of the area once occupied by the streets, temples and churches of Capitolias. Many of the houses have some beautifully carved stones built into them; rock-cut tombs with huge basalt doors, carved and inscribed, are used as stores for grain and straw, and cattle feed or drink out of the sarcophagi. The large Roman water cisterns are almost filled up with soil and a few fruit trees are planted in them, for in spite of inattention some water still insists on collecting in them each year.

Irbid lies on the western edge of a great plain which is wonderful cornland, stretching far away to the east, merging almost imperceptibly with the desert. In addition to a number of tracks of varying degrees of roughness connecting the town with the villages which are so numerous in this district, five larger roads radiate off in all directions. That to the east is at present the main road to Amman via Mafraq, though its place is likely to be taken by the road via Jarash when that is completed. Two roads lead off to the south, one to Jarash via Al Husn, the other direct to Ajlun. The one running west used to be the road to Haifa, but now goes as far as the Jordan valley only. It is very beautiful in the spring, when the flowers are in bloom, for it twists and turns its way down the mountainside through a series of natural rock gardens. About three miles along this road from Irbid, after descending into and climbing out of a small wadi, there is on the north of the road a small artificial mound called Tell al Ashiar. The Tell itself seems to be of the Iron Age, though no excavation has yet been carried out there, but to the south of the road at this point are great numbers of dolmens, those strange necropolises of the prehistoric period. This is, perhaps, the second biggest field of them in Jordan, the most extensive being that at Damiah, which will be mentioned later.

TELL AL HUSN

At Husn, on the Jarash road, is a magnificent specimen of a Tell, named after the town Tell al Husn. It is not very large in area, but there are probably some 40 feet of accumulated deposit making up its height. We know from the chance find of a tomb in the vicinity that it goes back at least to the Early Bronze Age, about 3000 B.C., and there is plenty of evidence, in the form of other tombs and inscribed and carved blocks, that it was still in existence in Roman and Byzantine times. It is one of the candidates for the site of the only Decapolis city so far unidentified,

41

Dion; the other being Aidun, nearer to Irbid. The latter is nearer to the original in name, but is a small, insignificant site and seems unlikely ever to have been an important town.

QALAT AL RABADH

There is nothing of archaeological interest on the Ajlun road, though some of the views down to the Jordan valley are impressive, but at Ajlun itself there is a very fine Arab castle; it can also be approached from Jarash. The castle called Qalat al Rabadh (Plate 5 B, C) stands on a prominence above the village to the west; the road to it passes through the village, and cars can be taken right up to the gate. It is one of the very few Arab castles dating from crusading times, having been built by Azz al Din Ausama, a cousin and one of the most able governors of Salah al Din (Saladin) in A.D. 1184–1185. Its chief purpose was to check the expansion of the Latin kingdom in Trans-Jordan, both from Karak in the south and from Beisan across the Jordan valley to the west, and to maintain easy communications with Damascus. The following is a translation of an account of its building by a thirteenth-century Arab writer:

The castle of Ajlun lies between the district of the Sawad, belonging to the Jordan province, and the district of Sharat. It is new and small and stands on a projecting spur overlooking the Jordan valley, visible both from Jerusalem and from the Nablus ridge. The range on which it is built is called Jebel Auf, because a clan of the Banu Auf lived there under the early Fatimide Caliphs. They had doughty and restless Amirs who were at feud with one another because their families were at odds. So things stood until the time of Malik al Adil Saif al Din abu Bakr ibn Ayyub (Saladin's brother) who gave the district as a fief to Azz al Din Ausama, one of his chief Amirs. He at once began to build a castle to protect his governors from the Banu Auf, but they hindered him so much that he represented to them that he was building it merely to protect them against the Franks. Then they grew amenable and helped him to build it. When it was finished he invited the sheikhs of the Banu Auf to the castle and set a banquet before them, and when they had eaten he ordered his young slaves to seize them and lock them up. It is said that an ancient monastery once stood on the site, inhabited by a Christian named Ajlun; when the monastery fell into ruin, the castle took its place and the name of the monk.

It was considerably altered and enlarged in 1214–1215 by Aibak ibn AbdAllah, mamluk and major-domo to the Caliph Al Malik Al Muazzam. These enlargements can be seen on the plan, figure 3. The original building is in solid black and the additions in hatched lines. The gates of the first castle are at A, those of the second at B and a still later entrance at C. Built into some of the walls are carved blocks, one with a cross on it, suggesting that the Arab tradition of an earlier "monastery," which word is loosely applied to all kinds of ancient buildings, was correct.

With the fall of Karak and the Latin kingdom the castle was no longer a military necessity, and in the late thirteenth century it became an administrative center and headquarters of a governor responsible to Damascus. It was also used as an arsenal and storehouse, and in 1217 was one of the centers where supplies were concentrated for the relief of Damietta in Egypt. Probably the long, gloomy galleries outside the keep were storerooms rather than living quarters. Peaceful times soon caused a village to spring up around the castle, and the ruins of it can be seen on the adjacent slopes. In times of danger, no doubt, everyone gathered in the castle and helped to defend it and themselves. The Tatars captured the place in 1260, but were driven out again in the same year.

The town of Ajlun seems to have existed at the same time as the castle, for in 1300 the Arab writer Dimishqi found "fruits of all kinds and provisions in plenty," and in 1355 Ibn Batuta describes it as "a fine town with good markets and a strong castle; a stream runs through the town and its waters are sweet and good." The lofty position of the castle made it an ideal beacon station, and it was part of the chain of beacons and pigeon posts by which news could be sent from the Euphrates frontier to Cairo between sunrise and sunset.

Nothing is known of its later history, except that in the seventeenth century some very crude repairs were done to it. When the traveller Burckhardt visited it in 1812 it was still inhabited by "about forty persons of the family of Barakat," but severe damage was done in the earthquake of 1837.

The beautiful little mosque in the village seems to date from

43

the thirteenth or fourteenth century, and its square minaret has suggested to some that it was originally a crusader church. But in view of the fact that the crusaders never, so far as we know, captured either Ajlun or its castle, this seems unlikely. The name of the village across the valley, Kafrinji, indicates that there were some Franks or Franjis there, but they may well have been prisoners.

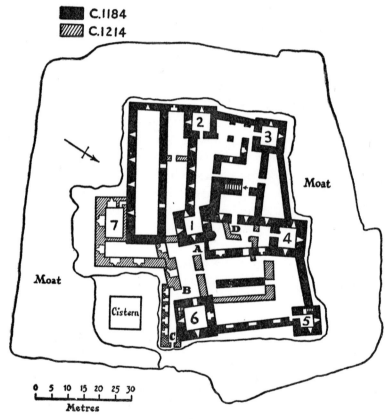

Fig. 3. Plan of Qalat al Rabadh

Considerable clearance and conservation works were carried out on the castle by the Department of Antiquities during the years 1927–1929, prior to which it was barely accessible, heavily encumbered with debris, and dangerous. The castle is now

44

entered by the third gate C by climbing up iron rungs set in the rock. When the dry moat or fosse was cut, a pillar of rock was left opposite this entrance, on which probably a wooden drawbridge rested. Climbing up the sloping passage one comes to gate B, with some birds crudely carved on the arch. There is a double wall above this gate, and in the space thus formed a portcullis was probably hung. Turning left inside this gate, then right again, one arrives at the original gate at A. Lying on the ground in front of it are two decorated corbels which at one time supported a machicoulis over the gate. The final entrance to the first building was at D, well protected by the towers 1 and 4 on either side. It can be seen from the plan that the original castle was roughly square with the towers 1, 2, 3 and 4 at each corner. The baileys were added on the east and south, that on the east having two corner towers, 5 and 6. The principal features which distinguish this early building are the roughness of the masonry and the narrow window slits. The later windows are larger, and the slit part sometimes contained loose blocks which could be removed for light and air in times of peace, a good example of which can be seen in the new tower 7. In addition to the large cistern just outside, there were others within the castle walls, some of which are still used.

AMMAN

Amman is the capital of Jordan, and the largest city in the country. It is also the only one apart from Jerusalem which boasts some modern hotels. It is a convenient center from which to make a number of short tours, and arrangements for longer ones can also be made there.

When I first visited it in 1932 it was little more than an overgrown village, for during Turkish times Al Salt had been the chief town of Trans-Jordan, and Amman was just another Circassian settlement. It was the Amir AbdAllah who, when he became ruler of the country after the First World War, made Amman the capital city of the new state, and it was a much better choice, for Amman is more centrally situated and has the advantage of a railway station. In 1932 many of the Circassian houses, both red-tiled and flat-roofed, were still to be seen, and the main part of the town lay in the valleys, though residential areas were beginning to creep up to the tops of the surrounding hills. Streets were narrow and mostly unpaved; the chief minister's office was in a little building down by the river, and the Amir AbdAllah's office was in a house beside the Philadelphia Hotel, then newly built. The shops and markets were still those of an eastern town on the fringe of the desert. The only road out to the south still crossed the stream by the Roman bridge, and many minor Roman and Byzantine remains were visible in various parts of the town. The Department of Antiquities was in a small five-roomed house adjoining the Roman theater. In Turkish times it had been the administrative center of the district, a function which it retained for a short time after the First World War, before becoming the first headquarters of the newly formed Arab Legion for a time, and finally the office of the Department of Antiquities.

When in 1936 I went to Jordan in charge of this department I lived first at Jarash, but with the outbreak of war in 1939 I had to move to Amman to cope with the various wartime jobs that were bestowed upon me, and remained there until 1956. The war brought great prosperity to the town, and residential areas began to spread farther and farther out from the center. Towards the end of the war the growth was so rapid that I often lost myself in some areas which I did not visit regularly. But the period of greatest growth came with the arrival in 1948–1949 of the refugees from Palestine, when both professional men and artisans set up in business there and built themselves houses. Now it is a large, prosperous but new city, and if the architecture of some of the buildings leaves something to be desired, the white limestone which is the chief building material is so beautiful in itself that there is no effect of shoddiness or vulgarity anywhere. There is still a part of the market devoted to the desert dweller and the peasants, but in the main shopping center goods from all over the world are on sale. The area covered by the modern city

46

is at least six times as great as that occupied by the Roman and Byzantine cities at the height of their prosperity.

History

The little excavation that has been carried out at Amman has been confined to the Citadel, where practically nothing earlier than the Roman period is left, and to the clearance by the Department of Antiquities of some tombs of the Bronze and Iron Ages and the Roman and Byzantine periods which have been discovered in the course of building operations. From remains in the vicinity, however, and frequent Biblical references, some of its early history can be reconstructed.

Flint implements found on the surrounding hills show that prehistoric man inhabited the site, there being a good water supply, which is a prime requisite for these early settlers. The implements date from the Palaeolithic, through the Neolithic to the Chalcolithic (about 3500 B.C.) periods: to the latter or to the Neolithic period belong the few dolmens still remaining in the neighborhood. Until recently there was a dolmen standing on the slope of a hill almost in the middle of Amman.

The Citadel Hill is undoubtedly the site of the ancient city so often referred to in the Old Testament as Rabbath Ammon, but most of this has vanished, having been swept away by the Romans when they began building on the site, and thrown over the edge of the hill. This was proved by the finding of sherds of the Early and Middle Bronze Ages, Iron Age and Hellenistic period mixed up with Roman sherds in deep cuttings made on the slopes of the Citadel Hill. That it was occupied in Hyksos times (Middle-Late Bronze Age, about 1600 B.C.) was further proved by the discovery of a tomb of that period to the southwest of the Citadel. The very recent discovery of a temple of the Late Bronze Age on the aerodrome shows that there was no lack of occupation in this period also.

The earliest Biblical reference is in Deuteronomy 3, which says that the great iron bed of Og king of Bashan is in Rabbah of Ammon, indicating that there had been a war between Ammon and Bashan in which Ammon had been successful and carried off spoil. It also shows that Rabbath Ammon was already (about 1200 B.C.) the capital of the Ammonites. In the division of the land among the Israelites, Moses allocated half the land of the children of Ammon to the tribe of Gad, though it is very doubtful whether the country as far east as Amman had actually been conquered, there being no specific reference to Rabbath Ammon (Joshua 13:25). Nor is it mentioned in the list of tribes and towns east of the Jordan in Joshua 12:1, though it is claimed that they took possession of the land from Aroer on the Wadi Mojib to Gilead and Bashan. Presumably only the western part of the country is referred to.

The next references give us more detailed information of events (I Samuel 2). Nahash king of Ammon, about 1050 B.C., made an attack on Jabesh Gilead to the northwest, the inhabitants of which sued for peace. He agreed to grant it on condition that they all have their right eyes put out. The elders asked for seven days' respite to try to collect reinforcements, which request was, strangely enough, granted, and they promptly sent to Saul in Palestine, who gathered an army and told the elders to promise to surrender to Nahash the following day. By this stratagem the Ammonites were deterred from attacking, taken unawares, and defeated.

When David came to the throne about 1000 B.C., Nahash died and was succeeded by his son Hanun (II Samuel 10). Nahash had apparently done some kindness to David, perhaps given him refuge on one of his frequent flights from Saul, and David wished to return this kindness to his son, sending servants "to comfort him" on the death of his father. But some busybody counsellors persuaded Hanun that David's intentions were not strictly honorable, and that he was only sending the servants as spies preliminary to attacking the city. So the messengers were seized, half their beards shaved off and the rear part of their garments cut away, which was apparently a customary way of expressing contempt for people. David was highly incensed at this action, and sent Joab with an army to avenge the insult. The Ammonites collected a number of allies, mostly Syrians, and "put the battle in array at the entering in of the gate; and the Syrians . . . by themselves in the field." Joab divided his army into two parts to cope with the situation and defeated the allies, driving the Ammonites back into the town. He did not follow up the victory by capturing the town, but returned to Jerusalem. The Syrians now summoned all their strength and gave battle again to David, but were soundly defeated and deterred from helping the Ammonites in future. Later David sent Joab with another army to reduce Rabbah. They laid siege to the city, but were not very successful, and it was at this siege that the disgraceful episode of Uriah the Hittite occurred. However, patience (and David's repentance) were rewarded, and Joab claimed to have taken the city, but, in spite of that, had to send for assistance to David on the rather slender pretext that if he took the city it might be named after him. David accordingly gathered further forces and captured the city. It is described as the "royal city," i.e., the capital, and the "city of waters," presumably referring to the springs from which the city's supply is still drawn. After taking the city David removed the crown of the king, which weighed one talent of gold and was set with precious stones, and put it on his own head. This may mean the crown from the statue of Milcom, the god of Ammon, which name means "their king." He also removed "exceeding much spoil." His treatment of the inhabitants was brutal in the extreme, as he "put them under saws and harrows of iron, and under axes of iron, and made them pass through the brick kiln," i.e., burned them alive.

The destruction was not, however, complete, for soon after Shobi, another son of Nahash, was king, and supplied David with provisions, "beds and basons," strange weapons of war, in his war against Absalom. Amman, in fact, continued to flourish, and when Solomon came to the throne he erected in Jerusalem shrines to a number of gods, including Milcom and Molech "the abomination of the Ammonites," and "so did all his strange wives" (II Kings 23, about 940 B.C.).

The next Biblical reference is in Amos 1:13 (about 760 B.C.?), where he prophesies against Rabbah, accusing the Ammonites of particularly brutal conduct in their fighting. He threatens a fire in the wall of Rabbah, which shall "devour the palaces thereof, with shouting in the day of battle, with a tempest in the day of the whirlwind." The king shall be carried away captive together with the princes, showing that there had been no diminution of Rabbah's condition. It is the first of a series of diatribes against the allegedly wicked city of Ammon.

At the beginning of the sixth century we find Jeremiah (49:2) saying that Milcom the god of Ammon possesses Gad, which seems to mean that not only had Ammon retained some independence but had even regained control of some of Gad's territory. Jeremiah prophesies, following the precedent of Amos, that Rabbah "shall become a desolate heap," and her daughters (i.e., villages) shall be burnt with fire, and must put on sackcloth and "run to and fro between the fences" because Milcom shall go into captivity and every man shall be driven out "right forth." Rabbah is rebuked for her very natural pride in her "flowing valley." All these threats are apparently in connection with the advance of Nebuchadnezzar of Babylon, who, however, did not oblige by fulfilling the prophecies. This may have been because Ammon was loyal to Babylon, as is suggested in II Kings 24:2.

A few years later, about 588 B.C., Ezekiel continues where Jeremiah left off, and threatens that Nebuchadnezzar shall destroy Ammon so that it shall "be no more remembered." There is an interesting reference to the king of Babylon coming to the point where the road forks, one going to Jerusalem and one to Rabbah: he uses divination to find out which road he should take, by shaking two arrows marked Jerusalem and Rabbah and drawing one forth, and various other methods. Apparently Jerusalem was unlucky, and again the prophecy against Ammon was not fulfilled. After the destruction of Jerusalem, Ezekiel is in a frenzy of rage against Ammon, whom he accuses of "clapping their hands and stamping their feet" and generally rejoicing at the discomfiture of the Jews—a natural reaction in the circumstances. He again insists that Rabbah shall be made a stable for camels and be occupied by Bedu. In 585 B.C. it was Baalis king of Ammon who for some reason incited Ishmael to kill Gedaliah, the Babylonian appointed governor of Judah (Jeremiah 40:14).

50

Thereafter the Bible is silent on the subject of Rabbah, and a few Hellenistic sherds alone show its continued occupation through the Greek period, about 300 B.C. From other ancient literary sources we learn that for at least part of the third century B.C. it was under the control of the Ptolemies of Egypt, and the city was rebuilt and renamed Philadelphia by Ptolemy II Philadelphus (283–246 B.C.). The Seleucid King Antiochus III captured the city about 218 B.C. after a long siege, which might have gone on indefinitely if a prisoner had not revealed the existence of a secret underground passage leading to outside supplies of water. Josephus, the Jewish historian, says there was only one small well in the Citadel, but we know there were also a great number of rainwater cisterns.

In the first century B.C. Amman was occupied by the Nabataeans for a short time, but they were driven out by Herod the Great about 30 B.C. After the Roman conquest, the city was replanned and rebuilt on a grand scale, erasing nearly all traces of its ancient buildings in the process. In Byzantine times it became the seat of the bishopric of Petra and Philadelphia, one of the nineteen Sees of Palestine Tertia which were under Bosra.

Excavations on the site on which the museum was subsequently built show that it was still flourishing at the time of the Arab conquest in the seventh century A.D., and the square building on the Citadel may have been built in the eighth century. A series of Arab travellers and geographers refer to the town during the succeeding centuries, and from their accounts one can trace a gradual decline in wealth and population, until in the fifteenth century it is referred to as a field of ruins. A small colony of Circassians was settled there by the Turks in about 1880, but it remained a poor village until the Amir AbdAllah made it his capital soon after the First World War. Since that date it has slowly grown into the flourishing city it now is, though once again in the process many of its ancient monuments have vanished.

The Monuments

There are still a few remains of Roman Philadelphia to be seen in the town itself, chief of which is the theater (Plate 6A). This is a large and imposing monument, built into the side of the cliff which was partly cut away to accommodate it. It could seat some 6,000 people. The stage and scaena have disappeared, only the foundations of the former remaining, and the orchestra has not yet been excavated; owing to the rise in level of the road outside, it would almost certainly be flooded in the winter rains. The few columns which are still standing nearby are part of what was originally a colonnade around a square or rectangular plaza, on the east side of which was the Odeum, now adjoining the hotel garden on the east. This was a much smaller theater which was used for concerts, recitals and more serious works than were performed in the theater; Odeums were usually roofed over.

On the banks of the stream are the remains of the Nymphaeum, which was obviously a very grand and important building; it is now very dilapidated, and part of its structure is incorporated in some existing houses. From here to a point somewhere behind the Philadelphia Hotel the stream was arched over, to comply with some now unknown aspect of the town planning. A small section of this vaulting can still be seen a short distance below the Nymphaeum. No inscriptions have been found on any of these monuments to give us a definite date, but judging from the architectural style they must have been built some time in the second or early third century A.D.

Like all other Roman cities, Amman had its paved street of columns, and occasionally when excavations are made for some new building a short stretch of the great stone paving-blocks is exposed to view, but otherwise there is nothing to be seen above ground.

The principal remains are on Citadel Hill, which was enclosed by a wall, some stretches of which can still be seen, especially on the north and northwestern sides (Plate 7c). Everything that is visible on the surface now is of the Roman, Byzantine or Umayyad periods, except at the northeast corner, where part of the Iron Age town wall is still exposed. The enclosed area was divided in two by a cross wall; the northern section is on a higher level than the eastern, and contains all the important public buildings, temples, churches, etc. In its present state it cannot be ascertained where the gates were, but there is one, of Byzantine times, in the west wall not far from the "square building" already mentioned. The best-preserved monument is this square building, which dates either from the Umayyad (seventh–eighth century A.D.) or from the Ghassanid period, sixth century. The purpose of it is by no means clear: it does not seem to have been a mosque, and as a dwelling the plan is singularly inadequate. It might have been a hall of audience, approached by the processional way from the living quarters to the north. Originally there was a dome over the center, and remains of fine carvings on the walls can still be seen (Plate 7A).

It is situated in the southern corner of what was in Roman times a large area open to the sky, surrounded by high walls decorated with shell niches; remains of the wall can be seen to the north and east. In later times this area was extensively built over, and it is these late buildings which are so much in evidence today. Outside the north wall of this open area were some large houses, perhaps the palace of the local governor and villas of senior officials. At present there are no visible remains earlier than the eighth century.

Immediately outside the Citadel wall to the north, on the land immediately below, is a huge rock-cut cistern in which is the entrance to the underground passage giving access to the Citadel, referred to previously. This cistern must have provided supplies of water for the garrison when they were besieged; the passage is now blocked by falls of the roof after a short distance, so it is not known where it comes out.

The Roman temple at the southwest corner was dedicated to Hercules, and an ancient tradition records that a gigantic statue of this god stood beside the temple. Tradition was right, for two fragments from such a statue in marble have been found, a piece of an elbow and a hand, from which we can estimate that the figure must have stood about 30 feet high. The temple itself was a fine example of its kind, for the workmanship is good and the plan solid. Within what was the cella the bare rock is exposed, and it was probably built on the site of earlier temples in which the rock represented the altar and high place. There is a suggestion that a flight of steps led from the temple to the town below, where in 1911 there were still remains of a propylaeum or ornamental gateway.

A very poorly built church of the sixth or seventh century is the only other monument now visible on the Citadel, but a glance at the hills around will show many caves, some now inhabited, which were the burying grounds and tombs of the old city. The big circular shaft near the square building was either a cistern itself, or possibly the other end of the underground tunnel referred to above.

A few miles north of Amman, on the old Roman road to Jarash, is a fine Roman family tomb, well built and decorated, called Qasr Nueijis, probably of the third century A.D. It is an attractive monument, but access is difficult.

On the tops of many of the hills round about Amman can be seen the ruins of very small, usually square, buildings and sometimes a stretch of walling. These are mostly of the Iron Age, and seem to represent a chain of watchtowers or forts all around the capital, from which ample warning could have been given of the approach of an enemy from any direction, and which could even have held up the attack for a while.

ARAQ AL AMIR

The ruins of this curious building lie in the valley of Wadi Sir to the west of Amman, and for those who enjoy riding it is a most delightful trip. Horses can be hired at Wadi Sir village, but it is best to make arrangements for this the day before.

The track leads out of the village to the west, on the south side of the valley, and soon begins to wind steeply downhill. The whole valley is a most lovely sight in spring, with tall trees growing on the banks of the stream and a green carpet of flowers and sprouting corn stretching over the hillside. In summer it appears even more attractive, when all around is parched and bare and one can sit in the leafy shade beside the running water. Even the somewhat taciturn Colonel Conder, who explored the country in

1881, wrote lyrically about this valley. These are his words, as recorded in his book *Heth and Moab:*

The scenery in this, and in the other gorges near it, presents a striking contrast to that of the plateau. Clear brooks are running between lawns of turf, or breaking in falls over high precipices, hung with brambles, and green with fern: thick oak woods of most English character climb the slopes, and here and there crown a white chalk-cliff. Lower down are yellow, red and purple sandstones, the peaks and narrow ridges of the marl just over the Jordan plains, broad wolds, dotted with trees and with Arab encampments, and the deep ravines, each with a narrow bed, in which the murmur of the stream is heard, but its course is concealed by the tall canes, or by the dusky oleander bushes, blushing with ruddy blossom.

The oak woods, alas, no longer climb the slopes, but the rest of his description still holds good.

The track soon crosses the stream, and continues along the north bank close to the water for some distance. Shortly after the crossing a rock-cut dwelling (?) can be seen in the cliff face of the south bank with windows in the upper story. Inside, the walls are honeycombed with small square recesses, which have suggested to some that the whole building may have been a vast pigeon cote. It probably dates from the first century B.C.–A.D. The road begins to climb slightly and soon leaves the stream some distance below. Near the little village of Al Bassah is one of the last watermills in the country which is still in use. A small valley coming in from the north is crossed, and shortly after passing a big tree with some graves around it, Araq al Amir can be seen lower down the valley.

The path begins to descend slowly, and now caves can be seen in the cliff face on the right. These are in two tiers, the doors of the upper ones opening into a long gallery running along the cliff face, and two of them have the name Tobiah carved by the door in old Hebrew characters. These caves are now mostly open and empty, and in some the water drips continually from roof and walls, turning the floor into a pool. They are surprisingly large, but not particularly well cut; some are used by the villagers as stores for grain and chaff.

55

The chief monument is the building now called Qasr al Abid, the castle of the slave. There is considerable contention among scholars as to when it was built and what was its purpose. For the former, opinions range from the third century B.C. to the first A.D., and it has variously been called a palace, a tomb and a temple. The plan and architectural features have hardly any known comparisons, so are of no assistance in indicating either date or function. Josephus in his book *Antiquities of the Jews* (12, IV, 11) says that a certain Hyrcanus in the time of Seleucus IV (187–175 B.C.) built hereabouts a strong castle of white stone surrounded by a fine park and lake, and having on its walls representations of "animals of a prodigious magnitude." He also made in "the rock that was over against him" caves several furlongs in length: Josephus calls them banquet halls and living rooms, and they appear to have been supplied with water. The whole description fits the site wonderfully; and, further, its name, Tyre, is preserved in the modern name of the valley, Sir, the particular form of the "s" used in Arabic being in Hebrew pronounced "TS." Some scholars have suggested that the names which are on the caves, Tobiah (Tobias), indicate that this was the headquarters of the Tobiads, the Jewish family already mentioned who were very powerful in Trans-Jordan during the first and second centuries B.C.

The "representations of animals" are now sadly mutilated, and the whole building has collapsed into itself, due largely to the extraordinary method of building. The blocks of stone are enormous, some of them 20 feet long by 10 feet high, but only about 18 inches thick; they are set up on end on this narrow edge, and consequently must inevitably have fallen at the slightest shock. Inside can be seen the remains of columns and capitals, and in the southeast corner one of the upper blocks has been cut to take stone stair treads. Also there are two loopholes here, but these seem to have been an afterthought, for one of them cuts through the carving of an animal outside. The confused condition of the building makes it difficult to be certain, but there seem to have been three entrances, one each on the north, south and east sides. There was an enclosure wall all around the castle, and on

56

the north is a depression which may have been the "lake" or moat referred to by Josephus. On the south was a gateway in the enclosed wall, and from this a ramp leads up in a curve to the cliff face. Perhaps the most puzzling feature of this puzzling place is the pairs of upright stones set at regular intervals along this ramp, with countersunk holes at the top. It has been suggested that these were used in some way to help in the moving of the stones for the building; that they carried water pipes for the supply of the castle, and so on, but no satisfactory evidence can be brought forward to support any of the theories. Their purpose is a mystery, and will probably remain so, though excavation of the site would no doubt do much towards answering some of the questions.

MADABA

Madaba lies 20½ miles to the south of Amman, on the road which leads on eventually to Karak and Petra. From Amman the road climbs up in a series of steep zigzags to the plateau above, where it levels off; to the west can be seen the ruins of an Iron Age village, now called Ummal Swaiwin. To the east is the village of Quaismah, and a small square building can be seen to the south of it, which is a Roman tomb of the second or third century A.D. Just before crossing the railway line for the second time a road branches off to the east leading to Sahab and Qasr al Kharanah, and on the west after the crossing is a ruined Iron Age fort. A little farther on are the remains of another Roman tomb on the east of the road, while on the west can be seen sarcophagi and a few columns and ruined walls, relics of a once-prosperous and extensive Roman village, now called Khirbat al Suq. At Yadudah is a large natural mound crowned with an impressive, fortresslike building; it is called Khirbat abu Jaber, but the fortresslike quality is more apparent than real. The road now crosses a great plain of red soil which produces very fine crops of corn; in spring large clumps of the black iris can be seen here (See map on page 39).

Madaba itself is somewhat rambling and untidy, built on a Tell or artificial mound which conceals the remains of all the earlier Madabas. The town has a long history behind it, being first mentioned in the Bible in Numbers 21 at the time of Exodus, about 1300 B.C.; a tomb of this period was found on the east of the town a few years ago. It next appears in the list of towns divided among the tribes in Joshua 13:9, when it was given to Reuben. It was then an Amorite town, lying between Dibon and the capital Heshbon. It is mentioned in the Mesha stele (see pages 26–27), at which time it was in Moabite hands.

By Maccabaean times (about 165 B.C.) it had been reoccupied by the Ammonites, but about 110 B.C. it was taken after a long siege by John Hyrcanus. It remained in Jewish hands until the time of Alexander Jannaeus, and was one of the towns promised to Aretas king of the Nabataeans if he helped Hyrcanus II to recover Jerusalem. The Romans made of it a typical provincial town like Jarash, with colonnaded streets, fine temples and other buildings, large water cisterns and a town wall. It continued to flourish to the end of the Byzantine period. It was then the seat of a bishopric, and is mentioned in the articles of the council of Chalcedon in A.D. 451. After this it appears to have been abandoned, and the earlier monuments were seen by travellers in the nineteenth century, but when a Christian community of about 2,000 people migrated there from Karak about 1880, everything quickly disappeared. Except for one cistern and the mosaics, no traces of the Roman town remain today.

The chief mosaic, a most interesting map of Palestine and Jordan now preserved in the Greek Orthodox church, was part of the floor of a church and probably dates from the sixth century A.D.; unfortunately it is very fragmentary, but there is a good picture of Jerusalem (Plate 8A), and it is one of the earliest contemporary maps of the country, and consequently of first-class importance for the identification of ancient town sites. There are several other mosaics in the town, all now in private houses, but arrangements have been made with the owners that visitors may inspect them if they wish. The following is a list of the houses and a brief indication of what is in each:

House of Mitri al Masarawa on the east side of the town; a

small perfect floor with animal figures and a medallion containing a female head in the center.

House of Misaad al Twal, near the above; large floor, probably of a private villa, partly built over by the modern house. Figures of a man and woman dancing, the woman wearing cymbals on her wrists and ankles; also some animal figures.

House of Aziz Shawaihat, on the west side of the town: remains of three or four different pavements, one in the courtyard, all in a poor state.

Part of a very fine floor which was in a house on the south side of the town has been removed to the museum for preservation, as it was being utilized for the floor of a garage. This floor is made of exceptionally long tesserae or stones, at least twice the length of those usually found.

MOUNT NEBO

Mount Nebo lies to the northwest of Madaba, and is one of the alleged sites of the tomb of Moses; the other is on the west side of the Dead Sea, on the road from Jericho to Jerusalem. If the Biblical account is at all accurate (and it usually is), the latter site is impossible, unless one presumes that the bones of Moses were transported there at some time.

The principal ruins are at a place called Syagha, and consist of a church and adjacent monastery. This church is first mentioned in an account of a pilgrimage made by a lady called Aetheria in about A.D. 394. She describes a small church which contained the tomb of Moses, the place having been miraculously revealed in a vision to a shepherd. Nothing is said of the monastery, but she mentions the holy men who showed her around. In the late fifth or early sixth century a visit to the place is related in the biography of Peter the Iberian. The building is now styled "a very large temple, named after the prophet (Moses) and many monasteries which are built round it," which seems to imply some enlargement of the buildings seen by Aetheria. A monk relates to Peter the story of the shepherd's vision which first caused the church to be built, and both Aetheria and Peter speak of the wonderful view from the summit. The site is mentioned again in 1217 by Theit-mar, who says that while on his way from Engeddi (Ain Jiddi on the western shore of the Dead Sea) to Shobak he spent a night there in the monastery. A Portuguese Franciscan monk visited the site in 1564, but the buildings on the summit were then ruined and abandoned, though a small church at Ayun Musa (Moses' Springs), in a valley just to the north, was still in use. Nebo is mentioned in a document of the seventeenth century, but ap-parently the writer was unaware of any buildings or even ruins on the site.

For many years from 1933 on, the Franciscan Biblical Institute of Jerusalem conducted excavations here, and have revealed the church and monasteries described by the early travellers. The church is of the usual basilica type, and the raised platformlike structure with steps beside it at the east end of the south aisle corresponds almost exactly with the tomb of Moses as described by Aetheria. The excavations confirm that in her day the church was quite a small one, and that it was enlarged in the late fifth century. In the room on the north side of the apse can be seen a curved wall which was part of the original early building. It was completely destroyed, probably by earthquake, in the late sixth century and rebuilt by the year 597; this is the building which we now see.

There are remains of mosaic floors in both the basilica and the side room and chapels, but they were terribly mutilated anciently. Those in the chapels contained some of the best work, with some charming pictures of animals and trees. The chapel on the south-east was the baptistry, and the font with an inscription in Greek is still in position. In the apse and in front of the chancel are some stone-lined graves, which contained the remains of a number of bodies. Some had been disturbed in ancient times and some were intact, but nothing of interest was found in any of them.

The monasteries cluster around the church on the west, north and south sides, the largest building being on the south. There must have been a considerable community living there, judging from the amount of accommodation the buildings would have provided.

60

From the terrace to the west of the church a wonderful view across the Jordan valley is obtained, and on a clear day the towers on the Mount of Olives, and Jericho, can be seen clearly. The Jordan itself is hidden in its deep gorge, by which its course can be made out, but the feature which dominates the scene is the Dead Sea shimmering in the sunlight some 3,500 feet below. It must have been from somewhere in the vicinity that Moses stood and surveyed the Promised Land, for the Biblical name of Mount Nebo is exactly preserved in the modern name of a nearby hill, Jabal Naba. But of Pisgah and Baal Peor, near which Moses was buried, there are no modern equivalents. According to the Mesha stele there must have been a fairly large village at Nebo, for Mesha states that he slew the 7,000 inhabitants and dragged off the vessels from the altar of Jehovah; but he is probably referring to the village at Makhaiyat.

In the buildings erected by the Franciscans are housed the objects found in the excavations, which will be shown to visitors on request.

About two miles off the road to the south lies Makhaiyat, where there is a fine, almost intact mosaic pavement in a church of the late sixth or early seventh century, and the Franciscans who excavated at Syagha have also cleared this church and erected a roofed building over it to preserve the mosaic. The whole nave is decorated with a vine which twists itself into circles, in which are human and animal figures. Men are represented as gathering and treading out the grapes, while one plays on a flute to celebrate so happy an occasion. In front of the chancel is a long inscription giving the dedication to St. Lot and St. Procopius, and the name of the founders Stephen and Elia, children of Comitissa, and "for the repose of John Anastasia and those who have contributed, whose names the Lord knows." Between the columns are various subjects; aquatic scenes, mythological beasts, and a church beside a river or sea, in which a man is very successfully fishing. In front of the entrance is a fine scene of bulls on either side of a fire altar with trees in the background. Sheep on either side of a tree are represented in the apse, a very popular ecclesiastical motif in the late periods.

From Madaba another road runs slightly southwest to the hot springs of Zarka Main, the Callirhoe of classical times. They lie in the deep and very steep gorge of the Wadi Zarka Main, and consist of a series of small and large pools of temperatures varying from one in which you could boil an egg to one in which you can comfortably and happily immerse yourself. A remarkable feature is the hot waterfall which pours into the largest of the pools. These springs were famous in Roman times, though there are practically no signs of ancient remains there; they were the springs to which Herod the Great used to descend from his palace at Machaerus on the mountain top to the south to treat the various diseases from which he apparently suffered.

Chapter IV

THERE ARE three great cities of the classical period in
the Middle East, Palmyra, Jarash and Petra, the former being
in Syria and the two latter in Jordan. Each has its own archaeological, historical and architectural interests, and each has
its individual type of attraction for the visitor. The setting of
each is equally individual, Palmyra on the edge of the desert,
Jarash in a well-watered valley and Petra among the sandstone
mountains of Edom. Of the three, Jarash alone is a typical
Roman provincial town, both in its plan and its architecture, and
is perhaps the best and most completely preserved example of
such in the Middle East. Palmyra and Petra both display many
features peculiar to the people who designed and built them, but
Jarash was clearly planned and designed as a unit by a Roman
architect, and the building must have been carried out under
Roman supervision, though no doubt most of the workers were
local. A vast army of masons and sculptors would have been
engaged on the project, to say nothing of those who hewed the
stone from the local quarries, for the greater part of what we see
today was planned and built within a comparatively short space
of time (see plan on page 75).

The ruins lie in a valley set in the heart of the mountains of
Gilead, about an hour and a quarter by car from Amman by the

new road. The valley runs approximately north and south, and while to the north the hills draw together and enclose the area, to the south they open out, and on the far skyline can be glimpsed the village of Swailah, which lies on the road from Amman to Jerusalem. The setting is a great part of the charm of the place, for a little stream runs through the center of the town, dividing the eastern from the western section, and even in the heat of summer, when the surrounding hills are brown and arid, the walnut and poplar trees which line its banks are always green and pleasant to the eye. The modern village is situated entirely on the eastern bank, and is inhabited mostly by Circassians, who were installed there by the Turks towards the end of the last century. They are, almost needless to say, experts in the handling of large stones, and while in early days their skill was used destructively, since the end of the First World War many have been employed on government projects of restoration and reconstruction, where their ability has been invaluable. A house with a round tower in the corner of the Artemis courtyard was built by the Turks to control the local population, and in those days was the government offices, police post, prison and stables, while another new house among the ruins, on a hillock east of the Forum, was built by the combined American and English expedition when they were excavating there in the 1930s.

The ruins of Jarash were rediscovered to the west by the German traveller Seetzen in 1806, and ever since that time the number of visitors, scholars and travellers has steadily increased. Archaeologically speaking, of course, the remains are comparatively recent, for there is nothing visible now that dates before the Christian era. But there is ample evidence that the site was occupied even as far back as the prehistoric period, as is indeed only to be expected of a place with such a fine permanent water supply. The surprising thing is that there seem to have been gaps in the occupation, or at any rate periods when it was not great enough to leave any traces. It is to the last of these blank periods, which dates from about the thirteenth century A.D. to the founding of the modern village in 1878, that the place owes its good state of preservation, inasmuch as the absence of any village or

64

settlement nearby meant that the ruins were not used as a convenient quarry for nicely cut and dressed stones. Much larger cities, such as Gadara and Philadelphia (Amman), have left scarcely a trace compared with Jarash, for this very reason. Fortunately, too, the village was sited on the east bank, where there do not appear to have been any large public buildings, and has been there too short a time to do any really serious damage, though the traveller Schumacher, who was there in 1891, describes how the Circassians were going along the main street of columns placing charges of gunpowder under them and blowing down column after column in order to find a drum of exactly the size they wanted.

The wealth of Jarash in its heyday must have been considerable, and would seem to have derived mainly from agricultural sources, there being good cornlands immediately to the east, for it is not on any particular trade route nor is it especially well placed strategically. It is possible that the iron mines in the Ajlun hills to the west may have had something to do with it, and an Arab writer of the thirteenth century A.D. says it was noted then for its fine daggers. Estimating from the population of the present village and the area it covers, the maximum population of the ancient town must have been between 13,000 and 18,000, though such an estimate can be no more than a good guess. The walls which enclosed the town, and which can still be seen for the greater part of their length, were, by the nature of their light construction, not intended to withstand a serious siege, but rather to keep off the desert marauders, who were a continual menace to settled life.

When, after the First World War, Jordan became part of the British Mandate for Palestine, the Department of Antiquities began to take an active interest in the site, and since about 1920 a great deal of excavation, conservation and reconstruction has been carried out. Before that date, to quote but one example, the Forum and the main street were completely buried under debris, and the difference in color of the lower and upper parts of a column shows to what depth it was buried and also gives some indication of how long that stage lasted, for patination of stone by

65

the sunlight requires more than a few years to take place. The great Propylaea of the Artemis temple was dilapidated and tottering, and was dismantled stone by stone and rebuilt, with new stones added where necessary. Much still remains to be done, but the government of Jordan has, since the termination of the mandate in 1948, been very generous in its grants for such purposes, especially considering its very slender resources.

The History

On the slopes immediately to the east of the Triumphal Arch a quantity of flint implements have been found, including some fine small hand axes, the presence of which indicates that here was at least part of the site of Neolithic Jarash, about 6000 B.C. It is probable, too, that the natural caves overlooking the stream here were also occupied in this period, as they are occasionally today. To the northeast of the town, where the municipal watertank now stands, is the site of an Early Bronze Age village, from which, at the time of the building of the tank, were recovered sherds, flints and other objects typical of the period, about 2500 B.C. On the hilltops above are the ruined remains of some dolmens, which belong to either the Chalcolithic or late Neolithic culture, about 4000 B.C.: the settlement of this period has not yet been found. There are now no visible remains of any settlement or village subsequent to the Early Bronze Age actually on the site, though, had such been situated where the Roman town now lies, they would have been swept away or buried when that was laid out.

Exactly when Jarash began to emerge from the obscurity of a small village to the importance of a Hellenistic town cannot now be determined, though this could not have taken place before the fourth century B.C. Inscriptions tell us that the town was at one time called Antioch on the Chrysorhoas (the early form of the present name was Gerasa), the latter, meaning "Golden River," being the somewhat grandiose name given to the little stream which still flows through the valley. The name Antioch is perhaps significant, and suggests that it may have been one of the Seleucid kings with the name Antiochus who was responsible for

66

the transformation. If this was so, then it was probably Antiochus IV in the early second century B.C., for we know he was active in Jordan. Other inscriptions, however, show that there were many traditions current as to the founding of the town; by some it is attributed to Alexander the Great, by others to his general Perdiccas, both in the fourth century B.C. Another possible candidate for the honor is Ptolemy II Philadelphus of Egypt (283–246 B.C.), who conquered and ruled the country for a time, rebuilding and renaming Amman as Philadelphia, after his own name. But it is probable that each of these made some contribution to the change, and that the emergence of Jarash from the chrysalis village of mud huts to the brightly colored butterfly of a Hellenistic town was due to increasing prosperity and security rather than to the efforts of any one ruler.

There is no historical mention of Jarash until the end of the second century B.C., when the historian Josephus refers to it as the place to which Theodosus, the "Tyrant" of Philadelphia, removed his treasure for safe keeping in the temple of Zeus when he had been turned out of Gadara. It appears that in those times the Zeus temple was an inviolable sanctuary, and any person taking refuge there, or any articles laid up for safe keeping, were free from molestation or theft so long as they remained within the precincts. Soon after this episode, however, Theodosus lost Jarash to Alexander Jannaeus, the Jewish high priest and ruler (102–76 B.C.), and it appears to have remained in Jewish hands until the coming of the Roman general Pompey. No doubt it suffered its share of the bickering and quarrelling which went on almost continuously among the petty Jewish rulers of the time.

Of the Hellenistic town there are now no remains to be seen, but traces of it were found in the course of excavation in the area of the South Tetrapylon, which indicated that the main street was on a different line from the later Roman one. That and the texts are at present the only evidence for its existence, apart from the discovery of an occasional coin or sherd of the period, and indeed except for the reference to the temple of Zeus we have no idea of the nature of the buildings which existed then. Certain inscriptions found in the neighborhood of the Forum and the

Zeus temple show that in the first, and probably in the second century B.C. also, the town extended from there to what is now the cathedral area, while yet others suggest that it may have included the area of the Artemis temple as well. Until further excavation is carried out, however, nothing more can be said about the town of the pre-Christian era.

In the year 63 B.C. occurred an event which changed the course of history not merely for Jarash but for the whole of the Near East, for in that year Pompey completed his conquest of the greater part of the area and proceeded to divide it up for purposes of administration into provinces. In this division Jarash and its lands were attached to the province of Syria.

This was the great turning point in the history of the town, and was recognized as such in its calendar, for to the very end of its life as an outpost of western civilization all dates are given in the Pompeian era. Under Hellenistic administration cities had enjoyed certain rights of self-government, and this policy was wisely continued under the new administration. Jarash had enjoyed these rights, and early in the Roman period of its history it joined the league of free cities known as the Decapolis. The greatest benefit conferred on its provinces and colonies by the Roman rule was perhaps the Pax Romana, which ensured a degree of security never before experienced in the Middle East. The effect on Jarash of this security—the prime essential for growth and development anywhere—was that commerce and agriculture expanded rapidly; people were able to devote time to the arts of peace.

There was a flourishing trade with the Nabataeans during the first centuries B.C.–A.D., and many coins of their king Aretas IV have been found there. Nabataean influence had already played a part in the development of Jarash, and stones carved in the typical "crowstep" pattern show that their type of architecture was known and used there. There is a bilingual inscription, unfortunately almost illegible, in Nabataean and Greek; yet others refer to a temple of the "Holy God Pakidas" and the "Arabian God." It can be deduced that this latter is Dushares, the chief Nabataean deity, and it is significant that both the inscriptions referring to him and the crowstep stones are found in the same area, near the cathedral and Fountain Court. There are remains of an early temple under the cathedral, which was in all probability that of the Arabian God, who was later identified with Dionysos.

A wise and apparently honest administration must have accumulated considerable wealth for the town during this period, for in the first century A.D. they embarked on an almost complete rebuilding program. A comprehensive town plan was drawn up, the basis of which was the typical Roman one of a main street with columns, intersected by two cross streets which governed the layout of everything else in the town. No substantial changes in this plan were made throughout the whole of its life. An inscription on the northwest gate, at the end of the north cross street, tells us that the enclosing town wall was completed in A.D. 75–76, thus setting a limit to the area of possible growth. A new temple of Zeus was begun about A.D. 22–23, and was still under construction in 69–70, the expenses of building being helped out by gifts from wealthy citizens, who seem to have taken a pride in contributing to the embellishment of their town. Next to this temple, the South theater was springing up at the same time, the older temple of Artemis was being improved and beautified by the addition of a portico and a pool; and in some unknown area a shrine to the Emperor Tiberius was erected. The main street at this time was bordered with Ionic columns, which are still extant in the Forum and the stretch of street north of the North Tetrapylon. In fact, the place must have been a hive of activity, and have been attaining a degree of wealth such as had never been seen before and has certainly not been repeated since that date.

This frenzied activity not merely continued but even increased in the second century, when the Emperor Trajan, about A.D. 106, extended the Roman frontiers, annexed the Nabataean kingdom, and built a magnificent series of roads throughout the provinces. More and more trade came to Jarash, more and more wealth was accumulated, and many of the large public buildings considered as the last word in the first century were pulled down and replaced by more elaborate and ornate structures. One of these was the North Gate, which had to be remodelled to meet Trajan's road, and was rebuilt in A.D. 115. At this time, too, many annual public festivals, athletic and other contests were inaugurated, and some inscriptions tell of the munificence of one, Titus Flavius Quirina, who gave banquets for both victors and vanquished. An essential feature of Roman life was the baths, without which no right-minded Roman could for a moment contemplate existence: Jarash had two of these, an enormous one on the east bank and a smaller one on the west bank. The functions of these institutions were much more than those of a mere Turkish bath; they represented the exclusive club life of the period, were not infrequently used to steam away unwanted relatives and provided an admirable setting for gay parties given by wealthy or merely ambitious citizens.

This second century A.D. saw the golden age of Jarash, when most of the great buildings one admires today were erected. The Emperor Hadrian paid a personal visit to the town, spending a part of the winter of 129–130 there, and his visit was the signal for a fresh outburst of building activity. The Triumphal Arch was erected to celebrate so important an event, and it would seem that there was the intention to extend the area of the city as far as the arch, for the ends were left rough, as though for bonding in to a wall. But no doubt the city fathers had enough on their hands already, and after Hadrian's departure the project was abandoned, and attention returned to the center of the city. Here a huge program of expansion and building was already in progress, which involved among other things the widening of the main street from the Forum to the Artemis temple, and the replacing of the Ionic columns with bigger and better Corinthian models. Marble was brought from Asia Minor and granite from Aswan for greater magnificence of effect. Temples were ruthlessly pulled down and rebuilt on grander lines, including that of the titulary goddess of the town, Artemis. The new building with its monumental gateway and long approach was dedicated in 150. The temple of Zeus was again rebuilt and dedicated about 163, the Nymphaeum in 191, a temple of Nemesis, now vanished, was erected just outside the north gate, and another a little farther up the valley, dedicated to Zeus Epicarpus, was built by a centurion.

Inscriptions of the period record the dedication by citizens of altars, pedestals, statues and stelae, and the erection of buildings now unidentifiable. Still others show that there were many priests of the cult of the living emperors, and that there were shrines to Zeus Helios Serapis, Zeus Poseidon, Isis, Apollo and Diana. The names of several provincial governors, procurators and other officials are recorded in other texts, and there is mention of the presence of soldiers of the third Cyrenaica and a tribune of the tenth Gemina legions.

The main source of water supply for the town is the spring within the walls, now known as Ain Qarawan. This is a strong, perennial spring, which seldom runs short of water, but as it lies almost in the bed of the valley it was too low to supply the needs of the great temples, fountains, etc., of the western bank. So a channel was built from Birketain, a spring about ½ mile up the valley to the north, and situated at a considerably higher level than Qarawan. There was apparently sufficient water here to supply the not inconsiderable needs of at least the western section of the town, though one does not get the impression that today's flow would have been adequate.

The peak of the town's development and wealth was reached early in the third century, when Jarash was promoted to the rank of colony, and on this dizzy pinnacle it poised for a few decades. Soon, however, the grade was steadily downhill, with an occasional level stretch or even a little rise, but the best was over. It was a gradual descent, closely connected with the fortunes of the Roman Empire, and for Jarash there were no precipices on the road. The spate of building activity ceased, whether gradually or abruptly it is difficult to tell, but there are many details of carving and decoration which have been left forever unfinished. By the end of the third century we begin to find carved and even inscribed blocks being carelessly re-used in building, which is always a bad sign.

The destruction of Palmyra in the north and the growth of the Sassanian kingdom in Iraq effectively put a stop to big-scale commerce, desert trade routes were abandoned and most of the transit trade now went by sea. Towns like Jarash, almost on the eastern border of the Roman Empire, must have felt the effect of all this at once, and furthermore, with the weakening of Roman power the old predatory instincts of the desert tribes came to the surface again and security became doubtful. But under Diocletian the Sassanians were defeated (about A.D. 300), and there was a short period during which some building operations, such as the circular plaza and shops round the South Tetrapylon, were carried out. The quality of the work, however, was slipshod, though not so bad as some of the late Byzantine building. Many of the inscriptions of this period were cut on earlier pedestals or columns or even on top of partly effaced earlier inscriptions.

By the middle of the fourth century there was a large Christian community in Jarash, and the cathedral and the Fountain Court were already functioning, for the fourth-century writer Epiphanius states that some of his contemporaries had drunk from the fountain of Gerasa, the waters of which turned to wine each year at the anniversary of the miracle of Cana. But from the town itself there is little history to be gleaned in this century; inscriptions are conspicuous by their absence, and the only outside reference tells that Christians were represented at the council of Seleucia in A.D. 359, by the Bishop Exeresius. Bishop Placcus represented them at the council of Chalcedon in 451, by which time Christianity must have become the ruling religion of the town. In 440–443 some repairs to the fortifications were carried out; the church of the Prophets, Apostles and Martyrs was built in 454–455, and that of St. Theodore in 464–466 when the Fountain Court was also remodelled.

Under Justinian (A.D. 527–565) there was a rise in prosperity and no fewer than seven churches are known to have been built in this period. Inscriptions record the erection of other public buildings of an unidentifiable nature, and even the revival of the pagan Maiumas water festival in 535. Many of the churches have been excavated, and from objects found in them and in related buildings we can get a good idea of life of the time. Low though the standard might be in comparison with former splendors, there was none the less a fair degree of cheap luxury. Appearances were all that mattered, and beauty was just skin deep. Gleaming marble and brightly colored glass mosaics on the walls of the churches concealed a type of construction than which it would be hard to imagine a worse. As life in this period centered mainly around the churches, it naturally reflected their style. The gaily dressed women who crowded the shops and drifted in and out of the churches were adorned with magnificent strings of stone beads and gold earrings and ornaments, which on close inspection turned out to be glass imitations and thinly gilded bronze. Still, it was all very pretty on the surface, and life was by no means unpleasant or difficult. There were baths constructed by the Bishop Placcus next door to St. Theodore's church for the use of parishioners, perhaps the earliest example of "cleanliness being next to godliness." The choristers had a club room just across the road from the church, and the clergy were provided with extensive and comfortable quarters adjoining the forecourt.

All this external beauty and comfort was achieved at the cost of the earlier buildings, particularly temples. An orgy of destruction of the pagan shrines must have gone on, and it seems as though scarcely one new stone was cut for the construction of any of the churches. The beautiful courtyard of the Artemis temple was desecrated by the building there of a potters' quarter complete with kilns.

The last church of which we know at present is that built by Bishop Genesius in A.D. 611, and the Persian invasion of 614 was the beginning of the end of Jarash. The only remains of this invasion are the socketed stones to hold goal posts in the Hippodrome, which was turned into a polo field. The Muslim conquest in about 636 completed the decline of the city, which, though it continued to be occupied, gradually shrank to about a quarter of its original size. A series of bad earthquakes, particularly that of 747, destroyed many of the churches and buildings, and as no one could afford to rebuild or even clear them, they were left exactly as they fell. The church of St. Theodore is an excellent example of this. None the less the abandonment and shrinkage was gradual, and some of the churches were still in use in 720, when the Caliph Yazid II issued a decree ordering that "all images and likenesses in his dominions, of bronze and of wood and of stone and of pigments, should be destroyed." The result of this edict is seen in the destruction of mosaic floors in such churches as St. John the Baptist: apparently the adjoining church of SS. Cosmos and Damianus was already a partially buried ruin, for the mosaic fortunately escaped.

This is almost the last thing we know of Jarash. Excavations show that the area of the Forum and the South Tetrapylon was still occupied in the late eighth century, but in the twelfth century comes the last known reference to the town. A crusader, William of Tyre, speaks of it as having been long uninhabited; a garrison of forty men stationed here by the Atabey of Damascus converted the Artemis temple into a fortress. It was captured by Baldwin II king of Jerusalem, 1118–1131, and utterly destroyed. The inner faces of the temple walls show clearly the effect of the burning which was apparently his method of destruction. Yaqut, a thirteenth-century Arab geographer, says that the place was described to him as a field of ruins, completely uninhabited.

So it happily remained until the settlement there of the Circassian colony by the Turks in 1878. To this day, Arabs as far afield as southern Palestine, when they wish to speak of something as extremely ruinous, say, "It is like the ruins of Jarash."

The Ruins

Appropriately enough, the first monument one sees when approaching Jarash is the Triumphal Arch, a triple gateway which is still standing to about half its original height. The central arch is 39 feet high, 21 feet wide, and 22 feet in depth, while the whole width is 85 feet. It was a gate of honor, in line with the principal entrance to the town, the South Gate, and was opened to admit great personages whom the city fathers wished especially to welcome. The semi-detached columns on both faces have wreaths of acanthus leaves above the bases, an unusual feature which is repeated on the South Gate. The large hollow to the west, almost adjoining and stretching beyond the arch, is a hippodrome with a semicircular end to the north. This was once wholly surrounded except on the south by tiers of seats, of which two or three remain on the west side. At a later date the hippodrome was reduced in size by the addition of another semicircular end at half its length. The road into the ruins now runs alongside it.

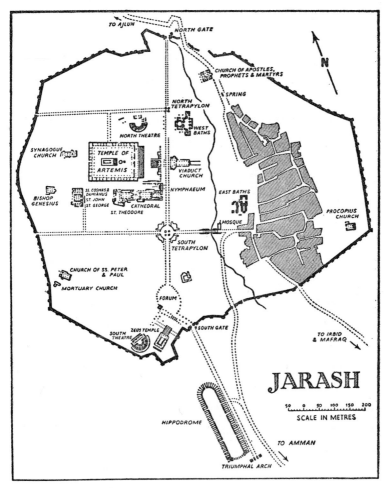

Fig. 4. Plan of the Roman city of Jarash

The South Gate, much destroyed and partly excavated on the west side, was a triple arch, similar to the Triumphal Arch, though much smaller in size. In the excavation can be seen the door of the gatekeeper's room; on either side are bastions of the

75

town wall. Beside it is the lodge of the present gatekeeper where entrance tickets are bought.

We now enter the town proper, and in looking at the ruins a few points should be remembered which will help the mind's eye to reconstruct and vivify the remains, such as that the temples all had pent roofs covered with red tiles; the elaborate carving of the capitals, architraves, etc., was painted in vivid colors, red, blue, green and yellow; the churches were nearly all roofed in the clerestory style; all the main buildings were profusely adorned with marble statues. No doubt many other points will occur to the inquiring mind, but these will suffice for a general impression. All the building materials are found locally in considerable variety, though granite columns and sawn marble slabs were imported for greater magnificence.

From the South Gate we pass straight into the Forum (Plates 9B, and 10A), which is paved in its outer part with large blocks of hard limestone, like those of the main street, while the center is paved with smaller blocks of softer stone. The Forum is of a peculiar shape, corresponding to no known geometrical or other figure. Evidently when it was built it had to be accommodated to some pre-existing constructional or natural peculiarity not now visible, though the approach to the Zeus temple must have been one of the features that influenced the design. The foundation wall on which the eastern colonnade stands is over 36 feet deep at the southern end. The capitals of the columns are of the Ionic order, whereas those of the main street are Corinthian; the Ionic order is found again in the main street north of the Artemis gate. The two columns at the north end of the east colonnade are much closer together than any others, having been moved to make room for an arch across the entrance to the main street when that was widened. This, together with the Ionic capitals, shows that the Forum precedes the present main street in date. The bosses left on the column drums were for holding the ropes when they were swung into place. The purpose of the stone chairs now in the center is not known; they were found built into a very late wall close to their present position, and may have come from the South theater. Near the chairs can be seen the remains of a square podium, which was probably the base for a statue. In Byzantine and Arab times small houses were built over the Forum, which had ceased by then to be used as a market and place of assembly. It was probably constructed early in the first century A.D., and names carved on some of the columns of the eastern colonnade commemorate public-spirited citizens who contributed towards the cost of the enterprise.

From the south end of the Forum a footpath leads up to the South theater, which was also built in the first century, but in the Corinthian order. A long inscription in Greek on the wall below the bottom row of seats on the west tells of a statue of Victory offered by a non-commissioned officer who had served in the army of Titus during the Jewish war in A.D. 70; it cost 3,000 drachmae and was put up in the reign of Domitian (A.D. 81–96). Some rough column drums, remains of an earlier building, are incorporated in the foundations of the stage. The back of the stage, or scaena, was originally two stories high, decorated with columns and niches containing statues; anyone who can remember the drop curtains of Victorian music halls will know exactly what it looked like. It has now been reconstructed up to the beginning of the second story, and though there is still a little more work to be done it does give a vivid idea of what the whole must have looked like. There were thirty-two tiers of seats, accommodating between 4,000 and 5,000 spectators; the lower tiers are numbered and could presumably be reserved. The acoustics are remarkably good, even today.

Adjoining the theater on the south is the temple of Zeus, and the present building was completed towards the end of the second century A.D. (161–166), but the site seems to have been a holy one from early times. Columns originally stood all around the cella or main building, but these have, with one exception, been overthrown by earthquakes: two on the north side lie on the ground complete from base to capital. The temple was approached from the Forum by a great flight of steps, all of which have disappeared. A remarkable feature is the huge vaults which were constructed to raise the level of the courtyard and to carry these steps. A fairly complete example about 100 feet long can be seen on the lowest terrace approached from the road, while others are used as stores for equipment.

We now return to the Forum and proceed along the main Street of Columns, which runs the whole length of the town from the Forum to the North Gate, a distance of some 650 yards. The original street was laid out between A.D. 39 and 76 in the Ionic order; the Corinthian order which now runs as far as the Artemis Gate represents an expansion and rebuilding in the last half of the second century (Plate 10B). Many of the square bases of the columns are unfinished, particularly those on the left shortly after leaving the Forum, and some of the larger columns are of uneven heights, necessitating an adjustment of the architraves. This also can be seen in the columns just mentioned. Wherever a large public building occurs, the height of the columns in front of it is raised in proportion to the height of the façade, as can be seen from those in front of the Nymphaeum and Artemis Propylaea. The street still retains its original paving stones along practically the whole length, and ruts made by chariot wheels can be clearly seen in some places, particularly near the South Tetrapylon. It is probable that the raised sidewalk, between the columns and the shops, was roofed in some way. There was a great drain running down the center of the street, with manholes at regular intervals; these had iron rings in them set in lead, and it used to be a favorite pastime of the villagers to chip out this lead for use in their old muzzleloaders. There were tanks and fountains at frequent intervals along the street, the greatest of which was the Nymphaeum. Holes can be seen in the curb for taking the rainwater into the main drain. In the center of the South Tetrapylon is the junction of the main street drain with that of the side street.

At the intersection of the main street by the two principal side streets Tetrapyla were erected, and the southern one (Plate 9A) consists of four square piers, each supporting four columns on top of which was a stepped pyramid probably surmounted by a statue. The southeast pier has been reconstructed as far as the bases of the columns, but the inscription on the south face is a later Byzantine addition. The circular plaza and shops around it were built in the late third or early fourth century, but we have

78

PLATES

A storm rising over the Dead Sea as workers excavate the site of the settlement of Khirbat Qumran; the mountains of Moab in the background

PLATE 2.

A. Pottery of the Chalcolithic period, when a wide variety of vessels was made, without the aid of a potter's wheel

B. Middle Bronze Age pottery showing a highly developed technique and beauty of form

PLATE 3.

A. The Moabite Stone (known a the Mesha stele) which was set up b Mesha king of Moab in about 85 B.C.

B. The Balua stele of the Early Iron Age. The figures apparently represent two gods and a king between them

PLATE 4.

Iron Age tomb finds. The daggers, and the seals and amulets (*top*) were found in the tomb at Madaba, the latter revealing strong Egyptian influence. The other photograph above is of seals from the Adoni Nur tomb at Amman and (*below*) the seal of Adoni Nur (slightly larger than actual size)

PLATE 5.

A. Shobak, an important Crusader stronghold

B. Qalat al Rabadh, fine Arab castle Ajlun

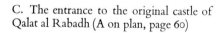

C. The entrance to the original castle of Qalat al Rabadh (A on plan, page 60)

PLATE 6. Amman

A. A view of the town from the Roman Theatre showing Citadel Hill in the background

B. A limestone figure of a king or deity found in Amman, probably late ninth or early eighth century B.C.

C. The Roman temple of Hercules on the Citadel

PLATE 7. Amman

A. The Arab or Ghassanid building on the Citadel

B. A marble statue from a group of Daedalus and Icarus, late second or early third century A.D.

C. Part of the Roman wall that originally enclosed Citadel Hill

PLATE 8.

Madaba. The picture-map of Jerusalem from a fine mosaic, probably of the sixth century Dhiban (Biblical Dibon). The Tall which conceals the site of settlements dating from about 3000 B.C.

PLATE 9. Jarash

A. The South Tetra-
pylon

B. A detail of the F
with the Temple of
in the background

C.
The Temple of Ar

PLATE 10. Jarash

he Forum and Street of Columns seen from the Temple of Zeus

he main Street of Columns. This section was constructed in the last half of the second century

PLATE 11. Karak

A. One of the rooms in the keep

B. The imposing castle of the Crusader period

PLATE 12.

A. Azraq. The Roman fort where Colonel T. E. Lawrence had his head-
     quarters during the latter part of his campaign

B. Dhat Ras. The small Roman temple

PLATE 13. Khirbat al Tannur

A. The Nabataean temple is on the summit of the hill on the left

B. Two of the stone carvings from the temple

PLATE 14. The entrance to Petra, called the Syk

PLATE 15. Petra
A. The Tomb of the Roman soldier

B. The Dair

C. The Palace Tomb

PLATE 16. Petra

A. The Snake Monument and an early tomb

B. Qasr al Bint, the Roman temple, and city area behind

C.
Early square tombs at the approach to Petra

PLATE 17.

Nabataean pottery found at Petra, which is as thin and delicate as porcelain and
reveals a high degree of technical and artistic mastery

PLATE 18.

A. The Hasma, looking across one of the mud flats on the way to Rum

B. Aqaba. The fourteenth-century Arab fort; the arms of the Hashemite family
are above the main door

PLATE 19.

Umm al Jamal

A. A private house in the Nabataean town

B. A view f
the North Ch
showing the t
in the backgr

C. A detail of the distinctive system of roofing

PLATE 20. Qasr al Hallabat

A Roman fort erected in the reign of Caracalla (A.D. 198-217) and later used as a monastery

The small mosque near the fort

PLATE 21. Qasr al Amra

A. A detail of one of the magnificent series of frescoes that decorate every inch of the walls

B. This beautiful building seems to have served as a hunting-lodge and baths (A.D. 705-15)

PLATE 22. Qasr al Kharanah
A. The imposing fort
B. One of the larger rooms

PLATE 23. Qasr al Tuba

A. A large but uncompleted Umayyad castle

B. Two doorways within the castle

PLATE 24. Qasr al Mashatta

A. A palace, probably of the Umayyad period. The whole façade was decorated
with elaborate carving, as shown in the foreground

B. The entrance to the trefoil-shaped room

PLATE 25 Jericho

PLATE 26. Jericho

A. A Middle Bronze Age tomb from Jericho, after the food on the table had been removed by the excavators

B. The finest Neolithic plastered skull, after conservation. This is one of the unique finds made at Jericho

PLATE 27. Khirbat al Mafjar

A. The entrance into the vast Umayyad palace which includes a mosque,
   baths, colonnaded forecourt and ornamental pool

B. One of the superb mosaics

PLATE 28. Khirbat al Mafjar

A. The floor of the baths is one of the largest single areas of ancient mosaic so far discovered

B. A superb example of the carved stucco from the baths

PLATE 29

A. Khirbat Qumran. Cave I, with the two Taamirah Bedu who first entered the cave. Mohammed al Dhib, the original finder of the cave, is on the right

B. Mr. G. Lankester Harding sorting fragments of Dead Sea Scrolls in the Palestine Archaeological Museum

PLATE 30.

An aerial view of Qumran showing the settlement of the Essene sect. The
numbering is referred to in the text

PLATE 31.
Khirbat Qumran

A. A view of the settlement from the western scarp with the Dead Sea in the background

B The caves where some of the Scrolls were found. Cave IV in the centre foreground, Cave V on the right, in the scarp of Wadi Qumran

C. Cistern steps showing the effect of the earthquake of 31 B.C.

no evidence as to when the Tetrapylon itself was put up. The cross street runs west to a gate in the town wall, and east steeply down to a bridge which spanned the valley at this point.

Continuing on along the main street, we next come to the gate and stairway leading to the cathedral, flanked on either side by shops. But this gate is really that of an earlier temple and beneath the stairway are remains of the original one. Next to this gate is the Nymphaeum, which was completed in A.D. 191, and functioned both as temple of the nymphs, who dwelt in water, and as the chief ornamental fountain of the city. It is built in two stories, the lower of which was covered in marble and the upper plastered and painted. In the upper part of the left-hand niche can be seen remains of this painting: green and orange triangles. There was a half dome or conch over the top, possibly with a mosaic decoration, but only a few fragments remain of the light volcanic ash of which it was constructed. In the niches of the lower story stood statues, probably holding vessels from which water poured into the great tank below: the holes of the water channels can still be seen. Surplus water from the tank flowed out through lions' heads into drains on the sidewalk, one of which is decorated with dolphins. At some later period a huge stone basin was inserted in the middle, though what purpose it served other than to take up room is not clear. The carving on this building is the most ornate of any in Jarash. Next to the Nymphaeum are more shops, one of which has an elaborate façade with two columns.

Then comes one of the most imposing structures in Jarash, the Propylaea and temple of Artemis (Plate 9c), who was the patron goddess of the city, her temple being the finest and most prominent building. It still stands majestically above everything else in the ruins, with its massive but beautifully proportioned columns which have survived so many earthquakes. But the temple itself is only the central feature of a grandly conceived and executed plan of courtyards, monumental gates and stairways. The whole dates to the middle of the second century A.D., the Propylaea being completed in 150. The plan began on the eastern side of the stream where a sloping roadway crossed the valley on a bridge, which is no longer there, though a part of it was seen and photographed by a traveller in the last century. What is now called the Viaduct Church is a continuation of this road, which was spanned by a triple gate standing where is now the church apse. The voussoirs, or arch stones, have been used to form this apse, and can be seen lying between the remains of the outer piers of the arch. This church is the only one so far observed which actually intrudes into a classical structure. A date of May 565 is given on a mosaic floor of the circular room on the north side of the Atrium; the mosaic is still buried. Very little actual building had to be done to convert the structure into a church; the colonnades and outer walls were mostly in position, and the fallen arch of the gate on the east made the beginnings of an excellent apse when laid out on the ground. The floor was already paved, and it was merely a matter of making the entrance narrower and roofing the nave. An unusual feature for Jarash is the thalassa, a receptacle for the water used in washing the sacred vessels and the hands of the celebrants; it consists of a deep basin cut in a stone, and the altar probably stood over it.

In the original plan the nave was the paved street, with a row of columns on either side, behind which was a blank wall; the space between was roofed over to form a sidewalk. Then came a courtyard of curious shape, later the atrium of the church, its western side opening much wider than the eastern, with the object of obtaining a full view of the magnificent Propylaea, the main street itself being too narrow to allow of its beauties being properly appreciated. In the street here lies a curious example of what earthquakes will do, for there is an arch and pediment complete, every stone of which is in position, though it must have fallen or been flung not less than 60 feet from either the Propylaea itself or the columns in front of it. Crossing the street and passing through the Great Gate, a flight of steps leads up to a platform. Here one was faced by the façade of the structure enclosing the temple courtyard, a row of columns with a blank wall behind them, pierced by a gate in the center. This wall was 394 feet long, and another flight of steps stretching the whole of its length led from the platform to the portico. A few remains of these steps can be seen in an excavation at the south end of the platform, which latter is now, of course, several yards higher than originally.

The courtyard itself was surrounded on all four sides by a wall and a portico of columns, those on the east and west being 528.6 feet long and on the north and south 394 feet. There was one entrance on each of the north and south sides, and the space between the portico and the blank wall was filled with rooms and recesses. The temple itself was approached by another flight of steps, now unfortunately disappeared, and there was a large altar in the courtyard in line with the axis of the temple. One corner of this altar can be seen under the Byzantine buildings, near the pottery kilns.

In order to maintain the level of the courtyard two large vaults had to be built on the north and south sides where the land slopes away. The southern vault is now used as a local museum, and houses some of the inscriptions, carvings and mosaics found among the ruins.

The cella, or temple proper, was raised on vaults in order to give it extra height, and the great platform on which it was built is 131.3 feet long, 73.9 feet wide and 13.8 feet high. The beautiful columns are 13¼ meters, nearly 45 feet high, and a row originally stood all around the cella, with a double row in front. Only those of the portico are now standing, and some of them are tilted considerably out of true; one of them actually rocks in a high wind, and the click-clack it makes can be heard for quite a distance. A final flight of four steps led up to the entrance of the cella, which is now blocked. The interior, like the outside, is perfectly plain, except for rectangular niches in the walls which were originally faced with marble. There are holes in the upper courses of stone which held the wooden roofing beams. The holy of holies was the raised platform under arches at the west end, and here stood the statue of the goddess. Only the priests were ever allowed into the cella, the worshippers having to stand outside in the courtyard.

The Byzantines built their hovels and kilns in the courtyard when the temple ceased to function, and stones, carved and plain, were dragged off to build churches. Finally in the twelfth century the Arabs blocked the main doorway, built walls between the columns and turned the temple into a fort. This was captured and destroyed by the crusaders, and no doubt much of the damage we see now was done at that time. Excavation here had been confined to a few trial trenches and pits, but they show how magnificent a monument it will be if ever the rubbish of the courtyard can be cleared away and some restoration of the building carried out. Access to the interior of the cella can be found through a little door in the south face, cut when it was a fort.

From the Artemis temple a good view of the city wall can be obtained. This is in the greater part preserved, following the slopes and contours of the valley on both sides; the east side is in best condition. The wall gives evidence of the growth and development of the city as it gradually increased in size, for on the west side it is extremely irregular in layout, not in consequence of the peculiarities of the site, but in order to contain and protect areas already covered with buildings. On the east side the construction is in long, straight lines. The whole work seems to belong to one period, namely the late first century A.D., as no variety can be seen in the style of building except repairs of later periods. In design it consists of solid bastions set at regular intervals of about 164 feet, square in plan, joined together by a curtain wall 8.2 feet thick, built of well-cut, large-drafted masonry on both faces, filled in with rubble and with earth thrown in. In intention, it is an enclosure wall to ward off raids or a sudden attack, not to withstand a regular siege with engines as there is no ditch.

Beyond the Artemis Propylaea the street narrows, and the Ionic order appears again. At the intersection of the north cross street is another Tetrapylon, quite different in plan from the southern one. This had four piers joined by arches, and the whole surmounted by a dome, giving an effect similar to the domed room of the baths adjoining. This Tetrapylon was dedicated in honor of Julia Domna, the Syrian wife of the Emperor Septimus Severus (A.D. 193–211). On the north and south faces were freestanding columns, and from the lions' heads on their bases water spouted into basins below. From here a footpath leads to the West Baths, constructed probably some time in the second century, and containing one of the earliest examples of what is technically known as a dome on pendentives, that is to say, a circular dome put onto a square room. There were originally three such domes, one on the large room to the west and one on each of the smaller rooms to the north and south; only that on the small north room now survives. On the west, the side nearest the street, was a fine courtyard with a double row of columns. But as no excavation has yet been undertaken in this building, and owing to its tumbled condition, it is difficult to be sure of the plan.

The North Gate, as now seen, was built in A.D. 115 under Claudius Severus, a legate of the Emperor Trajan who rebuilt the road from Pella in the Jordan valley to Jarash, replacing an earlier and less elaborate structure. A curious feature is that it is much wider on the west than on the east, due to the fact that the main Street of Columns and the Pella road meet at an obtuse angle, and the architect wished to present a façade at right angles to each road. About ½ mile up the valley from the North Gate is the spring which supplied the western half of the town with water. This spring is called now Berketain, the two cisterns, from the great masonry pool, divided in half by a cross wall, which was constructed around the spring. Adjoining these on the west is a small theater. A sixth-century inscription says that the notorious Maiumas water festival was held here, a festival frowned on by the Christian element, as it involved, among other things, mixed bathing. It is indeed surprising to find that it was celebrated here so late, and at a time when Christianity must have been very strong.

There was originally a colonnade around the pool, which must also have enjoyed a more sylvan setting than is at present the case. Even when Burckhardt visited the site in 1812 he described it as a "most romantic spot," where "large oak and walnut trees overshadow the stream." The pool was built in the early third century, and the theater somewhat later.

From the North Tetrapylon a street runs west, flanked by columns of the Ionic order, the tops of three of which can be seen sticking up out of the fields. A footpath leads past these to a plaza in the Corinthian order, with fine large columns and enormous architraves. Adjoining this on the south is the North theater, considerably smaller than the southern one. No excavation has yet been carried out here, and the date of these constructions is unknown, though probably the second or third century.

The only large remains on the east side are those of the East Baths, and these are in an advanced state of ruin. One room, however, still retains its vault almost complete, and is of vast proportions. It is used at present as a stable for animals, and can be approached from the main street of the village. No definite date can be assigned to their construction, but they are probably not later than the second century A.D.

Turning now to the Christian monuments, we have the remains of thirteen churches in Jarash, and it is highly probable that others are still buried, as towns far smaller had more than this number. With one exception, they are closely dated, and there has been no repair or restoration of the fabric since they were abandoned in the eighth or ninth century (some even earlier). They therefore represent material of first-class importance for the study of early Christian architecture, being of known date and in their original unaltered plan. Most of the inner walls of these churches were cased in marble, colored limestone slabs, painted plaster and sometimes glass mosaics; little but the holes into which the slabs were pegged now remain to tell of the ways in which the church was adorned and the poor quality of building concealed at one and the same time.

Probably the earliest Christian building so far known at Jarash is the cathedral, which must date from about A.D. 350–375; it is actually the only church which cannot be definitely dated. The evidence for its date is the presence of a bishop of Gerasa at the council of Seleucia in 359, and the record, as stated earlier, of Epiphanius, who, writing in 375, says that there was a fountain at Gerasa at which was enacted yearly the miracle of the changing of water into wine. This could only be the fountain in the courtyard west of the cathedral, and there is further confirmation of this in the fact that the cathedral itself is built on the site of a temple of the Infant Dionysos, and the wine episode is no doubt the transference of some Dionysiac rite to the rites of conquering Christianity.

The gate and stairs leading up from the main street have already been referred to; at the top of the stairs, against the back wall of the cathedral, are pieces of a small shrine dedicated to Michael, Holy Mary and Gabriel, whose names are painted in red on the band just below the shell. The columns and Ionic capitals lying here formed a colonnade around the upper part of the stairwell.

The cathedral can be entered from either the north or south, and in plan was of the usual basilica type, that is, a nave with north and south aisles and an apse in which stood the altar, a chancel enclosed by a marble screen and a pulpit at the southwest corner of the chancel. The columns and capitals, and indeed almost every stone in the building, were taken from earlier structures, the Dionysos temple no doubt contributing largely. In a trench in the middle of the nave can be seen a section of the podium on which the temple stood. The line of columns across the church at this point shows the size to which it was reduced after an earthquake in some later period. The chief feature is the Fountain Court on the west, referred to above. Originally this was a square courtyard surrounded by a colonnade with the fountain in the middle, but when St. Theodore was built, its apse and east wall jutted out into the court, and the whole of the western side and half the north and south sides of the colonnade were demolished. But the fountain remained, and the throne for the bishop or officiating priest is still in position on the west. The water was conducted to the fountain in lead pipes, which were still in position when first excavated, but have since been stolen.

On the north side of the court is a flight of steps leading to a passage which opens onto the road running up beside the Artemis courtyard from the Nymphaeum. A room to the right of these steps was used as a factory for the manufacture of mosaic glass in the sixth century. On the south side is a small chapel and "memorial of the repose of those who have contributed and of Mary," as the mosaic inscription tells us. It was probably built in the sixth century.

Two flights of stairs on the west lead to the Church of St. Theodore, built between A.D. 494 and 496. These dates are given in the inscriptions, one of which was set over the main west door and another over the outer gate of the church. They can be seen in the atrium or western courtyard of the church. The inscription which stood over the outer gate reads:

I have been made a wonder and a marvel at once to passers by. For all cloud of unseemliness is dispelled, and instead of the former eyesore the Grace of God surrounds me on every side. And once the baleful stench of four-footed beasts that toiling died and were here cast forth was spread abroad; and oft one going by held his nose and checked the passage of breath, shunning the foul odour. But now travellers passing o'er the scented plain bring their right hand to their forehead, making straightway the sign of the precious cross. And if thou wilt learn this also, that you may know it well, 'twas Aeneas that gave me this lovely beauty, the all wise chief priest, practised in piety.

The floor of this church was paved with slabs of colored limestone and marble, laid in patterns, but not much of it has survived. At the southwest there is a baptistry with the font let into the floor, and on the southeast is a small chapel with a mosaic floor. The atrium had a colonnade on three sides, and various small rooms, most of which had mosaic pavements. The complex of rooms on the north represents the clergy house, and on the south is a small chapel.

The columns of the nave lie exactly as they fell after some great earthquake, complete from base to capital with only the base in position. The destruction apparently was so complete that no attempt was made at salvage or restoration. The bases of the column drums have Greek letters on them, which were mason's marks to facilitate the assembly of the columns. As in the cathedral, all the stones come from some earlier building.

The passage on the northeast has a mosaic floor of red and white squares, and through a gap in its north wall can be seen part of the heating apparatus for the Baths of Placcus which adjoin. They seem at one time to have been stoked from this passage. The entrance to these baths is in the street running up by the side of the Artemis courtyard, and they were erected by

Bishop Placcus in 454-455 and restored in 584, as recorded in an inscription. Whether the good bishop built them out of charity or as a commercial proposition we are not told. At any rate he followed the tradition established by the church builders and borrowed all his materials from earlier structures.

A short distance to the west of St. Theodore lie the churches of St. John, St. George and SS. Cosmosand Damianus, which were all erected between A.D. 529 and 533; funds for the latter at least were contributed very largely by one Theodore and his wife Georgia. They have their reward, for their portraits and names are there in the mosaic pavements to this day for all the world to see and admire.

The arrangement of these three churches side by side, each opening into the other, arises from the custom of the Orthodox Eastern Church which did not allow the celebration of the liturgy more than once a day at any altar. In plan, the two outer buildings are of the usual basilica type, but the central one, dedicated to St. John, is a circle inside a square, with a square lantern in the center of the circle. The lantern was supported on four large columns, and the plan is an abridged edition of the cathedral at Bosra in Syria, built a few years earlier.

The southern church, dedicated to St. George, was in use as late as the eighth century, and is the only one of the three which still has the seats for the officiants in the apse. It also has two reliquaries and remains of two screens, which would seem to indicate that some church furniture had been salvaged from one of the other churches already fallen into disuse. This may explain the preservation of the mosaics in St. Cosmos, and a portion of them in St. John. If the former was already a complete, and the latter a partial, ruin, those who mutilated the St. George mosaics would not bother to dig out the others from the debris, and perhaps would not even be aware of their existence. The pavement of St. George is not particularly interesting (it is still buried), but St. John had a very fine floor with pictures of various cities, including Alexandria and Memphis. There was a wide scroll border with figures of animals and men, of which some pieces can be seen in the museum.

More than two-thirds of the Cosmos and Damianus mosaics are still intact, and they were lifted, repaired and relaid in a firm bed by the Department of Antiquities in 1937–1938. The figures are very fine, particularly those of Theodore and Georgia, though the former's head is a restoration. The inscriptions give the dedication and the date (A.D. 533), and below are portraits of other donors: John son of Astricius on the left, Calloeonistus on the right, and an inscription of the tribune Dagistheus (a general of the Emperor Justinian) in the diamond next to John. The remainder of the nave is filled with panels containing a great variety of motifs, including geometrical and interlacing designs, swastikas, birds and animals of all kinds. The space between the square pillars contained geometric designs, birds and fishes. The aisles had a plain carpet pattern, and the northern was very badly damaged and repaired in ancient times.

The three churches open onto a common atrium, which had a row of miscellaneous columns along one side. The space between the columns and churches was paved with mosaics, and the remainder with stone slabs. A stoup for holy water seems to have stood originally outside each church.

Of the rooms at the east end of the churches, that between St. Cosmos and St. John was originally a chapel, later converted into a baptistry. The font cuts through the floor decoration of a cross within a circle. Over the doorway in the west wall, leading to St. John's, is a large block carved with a lion's head and other motifs. This is a fragment from the outer cornice of the temple of Artemis, the lion's head being a water spout or gargoyle. Built into the floor of St. John's was a building inscription from the temple of Zeus. The other rooms seem to have served as sacristies.

The quality of constructional work of these churches is very poor, as can be seen particularly in some of the tumbled walls of St. George's. These consist of an inner and outer skin of stone, with the space in between filled with loose earth and pebbles. In the apse of St. Cosmos can be seen chips and fragments of stone left by the workmen who prepared the tesserae for the mosaic floor.

On the east side of the stream near the spring was an interesting church dedicated to the prophets, apostles and martyrs in 461–465, but now the motor road runs over a large part of it and nothing whatever can be seen. This is a pity, for it was unique in Jarash so far as its plan goes. It had good mosaics, and an inscription giving the date, last seen about 1860. Another church on the east was built in 526–527 by an officer named Procopius; remains of the columns can be seen from the western side, above the village to the southeast. It contained some of the finest mosaics yet found at Jarash, but they were badly mutilated and are still buried.

The remaining churches contain little of interest. That dedicated to SS. Peter and Paul, south of the St. John complex, was constructed about 540, and like St. John's had mosaic pictures of towns, though of poorer quality. A little farther south is the small Mortuary Church, built by an unnamed founder in honor of his parents, also unnamed. An arch on the south opens into a cave which was used as a burial place, probably a family vault. The church is largely excavated out of the hillside; it is undated, but probably is late sixth century. The Synagogue Church, west of the Artemis temple, is so called because the church itself was intruded into a synagogue in A.D. 530. This involved entire rearrangement of the plan, as a synagogue east of the Jordan is oriented to the west, whereas a church is oriented east. Nothing can now be seen of the synagogue except the columns, which are probably not in their original position. There are some mosaics belonging to it, with scenes of the flood and an inscription in Hebrew, but these are still buried. The church is otherwise undistinguished.

The Church of Bishop Genesius has the latest date so far found here, September A.D. 611. It has no other particular interest, and has not been completely excavated. It lies to the west of the St. John complex.

Chapter V

MUKAWIR · DHIBAN · MESHA STELE · AL QASR · AL
RABBAH · KARAK · MOTAH · MAZAR · DHAT RAS
· KHIRBAT AL TANNUR · DHANA · SHOBAK

THE DESERT ROAD from Amman to Petra is not much used by visitors nowadays, for it is very rough and dusty, there is almost no variety of scenery, and nothing of interest is to be seen in its whole length. The mountain road via Karak is now partly surfaced, and though the latter end is still rough, it offers some magnificent views and passes a number of interesting sites (see map III on page 91).

MUKAWIR

A few miles south of Madaba is a high, isolated hill on the west side of the road called Libb, itself the site of an ancient village, and immediately after passing this there is a track running off west which takes one ultimately to Mukawir, the site of Herod's palace, where one tradition has it that Salome danced and John the Baptist was beheaded. Cars can only be taken as far as Ataruz, from where it is a stiff walk to Mukawir. Apart from the magnificent view of the Dead Sea, there is but little to be seen, the palace—more like a fortress—having long since disappeared except for a few partly buried walls and the remains of a kind of causeway. But it is in a most commanding position, and from it can be seen Herod's two other mountain-top abodes: the Herodium not far from Bethlehem, and the Alexandrium at

90

Qarn Sartaba north of Jericho and just west of Damiah. The towers of Jerusalem are also visible on a clear day.

Continuing on down the Karak road, this soon winds down into the Wadi Wala, a tributary of the Mojib or Arnon; it is a perennial stream, fringed with pink oleanders, and with large fish in some of the pools. Soon after crossing the stream by the bridge, there is a solitary, standing stone or *menhir* by the side of the road, with some others, fallen, lying around. On the northern bank of the stream at this point is Khirbat Sakandar, a small ruined village of the Chalcolithic–Early Bronze Ages; the menhirs are probably related to this village. Near the top of the climb out of the valley can be seen a group of Roman milestones, fallen

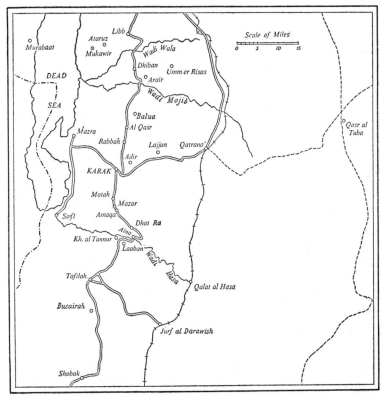

Fig. 5. Map III, showing the road from Amman via Karak and Shobak to Petra

91

but roughly in position, beside the old road and slightly below the present one.

DHIBAN

The next point of interest reached is the village and police post of Dhiban, with its imposing Tell slightly off the road to the west (Plate 8B). This was the site of the Biblical Dibon, one-time capital of Mesha king of Moab. The American School of Oriental Research has conducted several seasons of excavation here, and has shown that occupation of the site goes back to the Early Bronze Age, about 3000 B.C., though but few remains of this earliest town exist now. The whole surface of the Tell is covered with early Arab and Byzantine ruins, immediately below which remains of the Roman and Nabataean towns are found. There is also ample evidence for its occupation in the Iron Age. Ruined buildings, streets and walls of all these periods can be seen in the excavations, but it needs an archaeologist—one, moreover, who has actually worked on the dig—to be able to disentangle the various levels. In a large cutting on the east face of the Tell, however, is a short section of the city wall—of which period is still uncertain—beautifully built of astonishingly massive, roughly dressed stones, and still standing to a considerable height, although the base has not yet been reached. In the thickness of the wall, approached from the top, are two great shafts going down some thirty-six feet, presumably serving some constructional purpose not yet clear. It is one of the most impressive pieces of ancient city walling to be seen anywhere in Jordan. A few tombs of the late Iron Age, about seventh century B.C., have been found cut in the rock to the east of the Tell, but all had been robbed in ancient times.

It was here that the famous stele of Mesha was discovered in 1868 (see pages 26–27); this was found by the villagers, and word of it came to M. Clermont-Ganneau, a distinguished Orientalist attached to the French Consulate at Jerusalem. He saw the stone and arranged to buy it from the finders for £60, and, having first made a squeeze of it, returned to Jerusalem to collect the money. It was indeed fortunate that he made the copy, for no sooner was he out of sight than the families started quarrelling among themselves as to who was going to get the money, and some members who thought they were going to be deprived of what they considered their legitimate share surreptitiously lit a fire on the stele, and when it was thoroughly hot threw water over it. The stone being basalt, which is tough but sensitive to such treatment, shattered into many fragments, some of which were inevitably lost. What could be recovered when the scholar returned was collected, taken to Jerusalem and eventually to France, where the reconstructed stele can now be seen in the museum of the Louvre, in Paris (Plate 3A).

Soon after leaving Dhiban, the River Arnon (the present name of which is Wadi Mojib), is reached; both the descent and ascent are very steep and tortuous, and have given pause to many a good motorist. But there is a regular bus service between Amman and Karak which does the crossing twice a day without too much fuss; except, of course, when the river is in spate or a minor land-slide carries away a part of the road. The gorge itself is im-mensely impressive, being at this point some 2½ miles wide at the top and having a depth of about 1300 ft. On the northern edge of the gorge, about 2 miles east of the road, is a small site called Arair, which is the Biblical Aroer. Close by the point where the road crosses the stream are the remains of a Roman bridge. Nine miles after climbing out of the valley on to the plateau the village of Al Qasr (the castle) is reached, where there are the ruins of a small Nabataean temple. Some pieces of sculpture from this tem-ple have been incorporated into houses in the village, and show that it must have been of the same type and date as that at Tannur in the Wadi Hasa. The temple has never been excavated, and the interior is a tumbled mass of stones, under which may well lurk more sculpture. To the northeast lies Balua, though not visible from the road, where another stele was found some years ago (see pages 21–22). Three miles farther south is the village of Rab-bah, probably the site of the Biblical Rabbath Moab, Roman Are-opolis: some fine columns, part of a temple façade, peeping out of the debris and mud huts are all that remains of its past glory.

There are no other sites of interest on the road until the town of Karak is reached. This is imposingly situated on an almost isolated hilltop, and commands a magnificent view in all directions, especially towards the Dead Sea. Such a fine site must have been occupied since earliest times, though there is no actual evidence of such until the Iron Age, about 1200 B.C. It is given various names in the Old Testament—Kir Hareseth, Kir Heres, Kir of Moab—and was certainly one of the chief cities of the kingdom of Moab, even perhaps the capital at some time. The chief Biblical reference to it occurs in II Kings 3, when Mesha was king of Moab, Jehoram king of Israel and Jehoshaphat king of Judah, about 850 B.C. (see page 27). Most other Old Testament references are curses against the city by the prophet Isaiah. Little else is known of its history; in Byzantine times it was the seat of an archbishop and contained a much-venerated "church of Nazareth." Its greatest prominence was during the crusading period, when it was called Crac des Moabites or Le Pierre du Desert, and was the capital of the province of Oultre Jourdain. The fortifications were built in 1136 by Payem, lord of Karak and Monte Reale (Shobak). Its most famous—or notorious—lord was Renaud de Chatillon, who because of his treacherous habits was killed by Salah al Din after the battle of Hattin, on July 3, 1187. The town then passed into Muslim hands, and in 1263 the Egyptian ruler Baybars destroyed the church. Thereafter it passed out of the historical picture until 1840, when Ibrahim Pasha, in the course of his Syrian wars, captured it and destroyed much of the fortifications. After the First World War it became an administrative center under Mr. (now Sir) Alec Kirkbride, and at one stage even issued its own stamps. It is still the administrative center of a large and fertile district.

The present remains are all of the crusading period and later (Plate 11), the only material evidence of its earlier occupation—apart from occasional sherds and other objects of the Iron Age turned up in the course of road making—being the rear half of a lion carved on a basalt slab, and a headless bust of the Nabataean period. Both these pieces are built into later walls. In its crusading plan the town was entered only by three underground passages, one of which can be seen beside the present road just before it passes through a gap in the walls to enter the town. The chief point of interest is the Citadel, a typically crusader construction with long, dark, stone vaulted galleries, lighted only by arrow slits, from which large, heavy arches lead off into other gloomy rooms. Only in one room is there some attempt to lighten the somber effect; this is a small circular room which has a number of squinches round the drum of the dome. On the west is a neck of land originally connected with the battlements, but a deep, dry moat was cut through this, thus completely isolating the site. The sheer drop from these battlements is awe-inspiring, and in the good old days unwanted prisoners were flung from here to their death, having first had a wooden box carefully fastened round their head so that they should not be knocked unconscious before they reached the bottom. Such beauty as the place possesses is due entirely to the fact that it is ruined, for the crusaders, brilliant military architects though they may have been, wasted no time on frills and fancies, even if they had an eye for them.

From Karak the road runs almost due south for some distance across a high, rather dull and monotonous plateau. Ruins of ancient villages are scattered about the countryside, which is rich corn-producing land. At Motah, the first village to be passed, occurred the first clash between the forces of Islam and those of Byzantium in A.D. 632, when the Arabs were defeated and their leaders killed. They were buried in the next village, Mazar, where there is a very large and totally unexpected mosque, built over the tomb of Jaafar ibn abu Talib (see page 35). There was originally an early, probably twelfth century, mosque on the site, but about twenty-five years ago this was pulled down and the present one built. Two or three more small villages are passed before reaching the lip of the Wadi Hasa, but none of them exhibits anything of interest. Two miles east of the new road, at the village of Dhat Ras, is a small, rather well-preserved temple

(Plate 12B), probably of the second or third century A.D. It stands beside the old road, and in the village behind can be glimpsed a few columns and remains of ancient walls.

KHIRBAT AL TANNUR

Looking south from the point where the road begins its descent into the Wadi al Hasa, a change in the nature of the scenery can be observed; no longer is there a rolling plateau with smooth, rounded hills rising from it. Instead, numerous steep little valleys appear, and the hilltops take on a rough and jagged outline, which represents the change-over from limestone to sandstone rock. The view down the Wadi to the west is very impressive, and prominent in the mid distance is a high, isolated hill, on the top of which are the remains of a Nabataean temple, today called Khirbat al Tannur. The stream, which is perennial and as usual fringed with oleanders, is crossed by a bridge, and soon after passing this the foot of the hill on which Tannur stands is reached. It is a steep and arduous climb to the summit (Plate 13A). The temple dates from the first century B.C.–A.D., and is so far the only Nabataean temple ever to have been excavated. It has an outer paved courtyard, in the northeast corner of which stood a large altar; on the north and south are a number of small rooms, presumably for the officiants. On the west was an imposing façade decorated with columns and pilasters, in the center of which is a doorway approached by a few steps. Over this was a huge bust of a veiled goddess, surmounted in turn by an arch, each voussoir of which had a projecting horn; on the keystone was an eagle with spread wings. Other busts found in the vicinity may have been set into the wall between the columns.

Within the doorway is another smaller courtyard, in the center of which stood the shrine and main altar. This consisted of a square podium some 6½ feet high and about 10 feet square, the façade of which was adorned with engaged pilasters surmounted by a flat arch. In the niche thus formed the statues of the deities stood; one only was found *in situ*, that of a bearded male figure with a small bull standing at his feet, probably the god

96

Hadad. His consort must have stood beside him, but of her no trace remained. From halfway up, the pilasters are decorated with panels of alternating floral designs and female heads in high relief; these latter represent a goddess, and each one wears a different headdress. One has ears of wheat on her head, another has fishes (Plate 13B). She would seem to be the goddess Atargatis, and the two together most likely represent the local variant of the chief Nabataean deities Dushara and Allat. A flight of steps at the side led to the upper surface of the altar, where the sacrifices were probably made. The whole temple was richly adorned with carving and sculpture, most of which is now housed in the museum in Amman. Hauling these great blocks of stone up to the hilltop must have been a prodigious task, especially such pieces as that required for the huge veiled bust; bringing them down the hillside again was difficult enough.

The site stands at the junction of the Wadi Hasa and its tributary the Laaban, which was mentioned by name in one of the inscriptions found in the temple. The road crosses the Wadi Laaban, usually dry, by a ford, and after a short climb of about one mile a small heap of ruins can be seen to the east. These are the remains of another temple exactly similar in plan and date to Tannur; it has not yet been excavated, and there are most unfortunately some graves right on the spot where the altar stands.

There is now a long, steady climb out of the valley, and the road finally emerges onto a small plain, on the far side of which a turning goes off east to Jurf al Darawish and Maan. At this end of the plain Colonel Lawrence fought his famous battle of Tafilah, the one and only set battle of all his campaigns. Soon the road dips down into another valley, and after a few twists and turns the town of Tafilah can be seen on the opposite side of the valley, surrounded by olive trees. It is one of the most beautifully situated towns in the country, and from it a wonderful view is obtained northwest down the valley to the southern end of the Dead Sea. Otherwise it is of no particular interest, and the road merely skirts the edge of it and quickly climbs out of the valley.

From now on to Wadi Musa the scenery is magnificent, and in particular a halt should be made on the road above the village of

Dhana, from where there is a breathtakingly beautiful view down to the Wadi Arabah on the west, with the flat roofs of the little village of Dhana lying immediately below one. At this point, too, is a low rock scarp on the east of the road, on top of which can be found numbers of tiny flint flakes and implements of the Microlithic, late Palaeolithic, culture, though one can hardly imagine that early man chose the site because of the view.

A few miles farther on a fine stretch of the great Roman road of Trajan can be seen beside the modern road. It is part of the great paved way which ran from Damascus to Aqaba. Soon after this Shobak appears rather suddenly in a valley to the west, perched on top of an isolated hill in the middle of a deep ravine (Plate 5A). From the distance it is very impressive, but hardly repays a closer view. It was an important crusader stronghold, known as Monte Reale, and was built by Baldwin I in 1115 to control the road from Damascus to Egypt. Saladin captured it in 1189, and it was restored by the Mamelukes in the fourteenth century; it is this restoration which we now see. The circle of walls and the gateway are complete, but within is only the modern village, the sole ancient remains being a great rock-cut well shaft with 375 steps leading down to an underground water supply. The descent is slippery and hazardous, and how the ancient excavators knew they would reach water at the bottom is a mystery.

Soon after passing the village of Najal, the road runs through an area which is dotted with the stumps of trees, all that remains of a once-extensive forest. This was cut down by the Turks in the First World War as fuel for their railway, and the embankment of the light railway which they built to take the wood away can still be seen. Beyond this the road runs along almost the crest of the hills, which here rise to a height of 5,500 feet above sea level, the highest in Jordan. After a long, gradual descent, the road from Maan to Wadi Musa is joined, and soon the spring of Ain Musa is reached, which is the beginning of the approach to Petra.

Chapter VI

THE name and some idea of the nature of this unique
ancient site is known throughout the civilized world, but despite
modern communications it still remains remote and not easy of
access, though it is true that in recent years parties from Beirut
have flown to Maan, spent the night in Petra, and flown back
to Beirut the next day. But such a form of travel is only for the
fairly well off and is a very recent innovation. When I first
visited Petra in 1932 in company with some fellow archaeologists
at the end of a season of excavations near Gaza in Palestine no such
facilities were available, nor could we have afforded them if they
had been. Instead we drove in a station wagon—six of us and two
of our young Bedu workers—from Gaza via Jerusalem and
Amman, and except for a brief stretch near Jerusalem there was
not a yard of surfaced road the whole way. But it was an ad-
venture, with Petra as its culmination, and nobody was dis-
appointed or disillusioned. For Petra is everything that the travel
agencies write about—except rose red; mostly the sandstone is of
a dark red ochre shade, with fantastic bandings of yellow, gray
and white in some places. The only part which could be called
rose red is the Khaznah area, and I know nothing to equal the
first sight of this huge rock-cut façade glowing in brilliant sun-

light after one emerges from the darkness of the great cleft which leads into the city.

I have visited Petra many times, but always that first, breathtaking vision remains in my mind. Nor does familiarity breed contempt here, for at every visit one has to rein up the horse or stop in one's tracks and gaze astonished, as if seeing it again for the first time, at the sharpness and purity of line of the carving and the glowing brilliance of the rock.

But Petra really begins at Wadi Musa (the valley of Moses, this being one of the traditional sites where Moses struck the rock and the water gushed forth) and the village of Elji, for under this lie the remains of an outlying suburb of the city. The strong spring supplies all the water to the village, though none of it now reaches as far as Petra. It is possible that a good deal of the business and trade was carried out here, rather than that the great camel caravans should descend through the narrow, tortuous cleft into Petra itself. The first view of the area from the spring—Petra is invisible in the mountains—is astonshing and fantastic. The smooth-topped limestone mountains suddenly cease, and before one is a vast panorama of rugged sandstone peaks, white, brown and red in color, while in the distance to the west can be seen the blue haze of Sinai. Trees cling to the slopes of the crags wherever they can find a foothold and sufficient water to keep them alive, and the whole effect is strangely like looking at a Chinese landscape painting.

All knowledge of the site of this unique city was lost to the Western world from the time of the crusades, about A.D. 1200, until 1812, when a young Anglo-Swiss explorer named Burckhardt rediscovered it. He was exploring in the Middle East on behalf of an English learned society, and was making the journey from Damascus to Cairo, a very hazardous undertaking in those days. As he proceeded slowly down through Jordan, he began to hear tales from his guide and visitors of some extraordinary ruins hidden away in a mountain fastness. He first mentions it in his journal on August 22, saying he is particularly desirous of visiting Wadi Musa and its antiquities, of which he had heard the people speak with great admiration. He wanted to go straight on from

Wadi Musa to Cairo, avoiding Aqaba, but his guide insisted on taking the longer route on the grounds that the other was too dangerous. He says:

The road from Shobak to Aqaba, which is tolerably good . . . lies to the east of Wadi Musa, and to have quitted it out of mere curiosity to see the Wadi would have looked suspicious in the eyes of the Arabs. I, therefore, pretended to have made a vow to have slaughtered a goat in honour of Haroun (Aaron), whose tomb I knew was situated at the extremity of the valley, and by this stratagem I thought that I should have the means of seeing the valley on my way to the tomb. To this my guide had nothing to oppose; the dread of drawing on himself, by resistance, the wrath of Haroun completely silenced him.

Encampments of peasants were found at a place he called Oerak, really Woairah, the Crusader Castle near Wadi Musa, and by them he was guided to Ain Musa, the spring, where he was pressed to make his sacrifice to Harun as other pilgrims had done, for the tomb is visible from here, though very far off.

Having got so close to his objective, he naturally declined the suggestion, and finally in the village of Elji he found someone to guide him to the tomb of Aaron and also to carry the goat and a very necessary water skin. As he descended from the village, he noted that "Here the antiquities begin," but he was quite unable to stop and examine them because of the suspicions of his guide. However, he saw the free-standing square tombs and the Obelisk tomb before being hurried on through the Syk into Petra. Somehow he managed to get inside the Khaznah, for he gives a reasonable plan of it. His powers of persuasion must have been great, for he also got to see the tombs we now know as the Urn and the Corinthian tombs, from whence he crossed over to the ruins to the Roman temple. He was then, however, going a bit too far, for the guide started to accuse him of being a treasure hunter because of his curiosity and threatened him with his rifle. None the less, they continued on until they reached Al Barra, just south of Umm al Biyara, from which a good view of the tomb on top of Jabal Harun is obtained. By this time it was sunset, and being, as he says, "excessively fatigued" he decided to sacrifice the goat there and then. After doing this he had to return at once to Elji in the dark, and so saw no more of the ruins. But he deduces: ". . . it appears very probable that the ruins in Wadi Musa are those of ancient Petra, and it is remarkable that Eusebius says that the tomb of Aaron was shown near Petra."

Apparently one of the reasons the local inhabitants were unwilling to show the place to foreigners was that they were afraid that as a result a host of foreigners would come to the place and interfere with their, perhaps not always legal, means of livelihood. This was just what happened after Buckhardt had told the world of his discovery, though it is to be doubted if the visitors interfered much with the villagers' activities. Nowadays, of course, they will go to almost any trouble to encourage foreigners to come, for a great part of their livelihood depends on a good tourist trade.

It is only since about 1925 that it has been possible for any except very intrepid and wealthy explorers to visit Petra, for the local inhabitants maintained their unfriendly attitude for a long time, even massacring the members of the first Arab Legion police post, established there to protect visitors. Yet in 1956 Miss Diana Kirkbride was able to spend six months there on her own in charge of excavations, with no more trouble than an occasional row from someone who thought he ought to be employed on the work and wanted to know why he wasn't. The comparative ease and security with which a visit can now be made, however, does not make it in any way a less exciting experience; Petra is unique.

The History

The history of Petra is still almost as elusive as its site once was, though thanks to recent explorations by Miss Kirkbride we now know something of its early story. Traces of Palaeolithic man in the form of the usual hand axes have been found on some of the higher mountain slopes, but in a remote and very inaccessible valley in the heart of Petra Miss Kirkbride found a rock shelter of the Upper Palaeolithic period, probably about 10,000 B.C., where prehistoric man had apparently lived for at least part of each year over a considerable period of time. Characteristic flint and other implements were found there. There is also a little settlement of the succeeding Neolithic period on the road to the northern suburb of Al Barid, from which flint arrowheads, blades and other implements were recovered, similar to some of those found in the earlier levels of Jericho. Casual surface finds of flints have been made before in Petra, but this is the first time that actual settlements and dwelling places of the period have been discovered.

Of the subsequent periods, the Chalcolithic and Bronze Ages, no trace has as yet been revealed, and nothing further is known of its history until the Iron Age. There is good reason to believe that it is the site of the Biblical Sela, and both the Hebrew and the later Greek name, Petra, mean the same thing, rock, though in Arabic *sela* means rather a rock cleft, which is even more appropriate as a name for the place. It is in the ancient kingdom of Edom, of which the original inhabitants were called Horites or mountain dwellers, and were driven out by the Edomites, who occupied the country, including Sela-Petra, until they were in turn driven out by the Nabataeans. Amaziah king of Judah, when he had defeated the Edomites in a great battle, slaughtered 10,000 (or ten families, for the same word can mean either) of them on the spot, and took another 10,000 (or ten families) to the Rock, which he had captured, "and cast them down from the top of the Rock, that they all were broken in pieces." Some evidence for the occupation of Petra in the Iron Age (about the ninth century B.C.) has been found on top of Umm al Biyara, the huge massif to the west of the temple, but it would seem to have been a place of refuge rather than a permanently inhabited settlement. It must have been from the top of this massif that the prisoners were cast down.

The Nabataeans and Petra are bound firmly together in history, for it was they who first began seriously to settle in the place, and to evolve types of architecture, sculpture, pottery and stone dressing peculiar to themselves. Perhaps the pottery is their most remarkable achievement, though it is the commonest and was obviously not held in any special esteem by them, for it is of a thinness and fineness only equalled by the best porcelain. It is even more remarkable than porcelain in some ways, for it

is all thrown on the wheel and turned, or smoothed down after-
wards, whereas porcelain is cast in a mold; furthermore, the
commonest form is a shallow open bowl, notoriously one of the
most difficult forms to throw on a wheel even when it is made
fairly thick. The interior of these bowls is covered with a very
delicate decoration in dark brown or black paint, and the whole
style and nature of the work is so characteristic that even a small
sherd can be definitely identified wherever it is found (Plate 17).

Their method of dressing stone is equally individual; they used
a single-ended pick and ran the cutting lines at an angle of
45 degrees across the face of the block, column, rock face or whatever they were shaping. Many examples of this can, of course, be
seen in Petra.

They had also their own script and language; the former bears
some resemblance to the Hebrew script of the time, but is
curiously elongated vertically. Their habit of connecting some
of the letters together, combined with the close packing of them
due to their elongated form, makes reading of the inscriptions
very difficult. Also inscriptions unfortunately are by no means
common, apart from casual graffiti scratched on rock faces, and
the longest we know is contained in some Nabataean papyri
found in a cave on the shores of the Dead Sea east of Bethlehem.
One long Nabataean inscription can be seen in Petra, on the
Turkomaniah tomb. Nevertheless it was from Nabataean that
Kufic and consequently Arabic eventually derived. The language
was apparently a form of Aramaic with strong Arabic influence
in it; most of their personal names are Arabic.

The chief deities of the Nabataeans were Dushara and Allat;
the former was always symbolized by a block of stone or obelisk,
and the latter is frequently associated with springs and water.
Dushara or Dushares (the Hellenized form) is from the Arabic
Dhu-esh-Shera, which means He of Shera; the Shera are the
mountains of the Petra neighborhood, this being also their name
today, and are called in the Old Testament "Seir," which is the
same word. Jehovah is said to be "He of Seir," in other words
the same person as Dushara, and Jehovah also inhabited a block

of stone, sometimes called Beth El, the House of God, and had His chief shrines in high places, as did Dushara.

The Nabataeans themselves seem originally to have been a nomadic Arab tribe of some size, who occupied the north-western part of the Arabia, through which country lay the route of the spice and incense caravans from the Hadhramaut in the south. In the beginning they probably merely plundered these caravans and made off with the booty, but as they grew more powerful they seem to have levied some sort of toll as a guarantee of safe conduct. The first historical mention of the Nabataeans as a people is in a list of the enemies of Ashur-bani-pal, king of Assyria in 647 B.C., but at that time Petra was still occupied by the Edomites, who were not turned out of the country until at least a century later. Exactly when they first began to settle in Petra cannot yet be established with any degree of certainty, but the classical writer Diodorus Siculus gives some account of Petra, but quoting an earlier writer, which would seem to date about 310 B.C. He describes it as a "Rock . . . extremely strong but without walls," probably referring to Umm al Biyara, and goes on to give some interesting information about the "Arabs who are called Nabataei." Among other things he tells us that they had a law "neither to sow corn nor to plant any fruit-bearing trees nor to use wine nor to build a house."

He records a campaign by Antigonus, the Greek ruler of Syria, to suppress the Nabataeans, in which, all the young men being absent at a great fair somewhere in the neighborhood, his troops occupied the Rock, killed many of the old men who had been left behind, also women and children, and hurriedly re-treated with a booty of frankincense and myrrh and about 500 talents of silver. The absent men could not, however, have been very far away, for the news reached them within an hour or two. They returned, made a rapid survey of the damage and immediately set off in pursuit of the Greek army, which, not believing the Arabs could return so soon, thought itself quite secure from attack and had consequently been somewhat careless in setting out its guards. The Nabataeans attacked, captured and sacked the camp, massacring most of the soldiers, only fifty out of 4,000 getting away. When they returned to their Rock they sent a letter to Antigonus explaining the whole episode, as they were apparently anxious to keep on good terms with him. Antigonus pretended to accept their explanation and offered them friendship, while planning another assault which he carried out not long after with his son Demetrius at the head of the forces. The Nabataeans, however, were not deceived nor caught napping a second time. They maintained lookouts to inform them of the approach of the enemy, and as soon as they got news that an army was on its way they packed up all their belongings, deposited what they could not carry with them on the Rock with a strong guard, and dispersed into the desert. Demetrius completely failed to storm the Rock, and finally allowed himself to be bought off with costly presents.

All this suggests that in the fourth century B.C. there was no city proper in Petra, but excavation has revealed sherds of Greek vases which date to about 300 B.C., thrown away on the rubbish-heaps just south of the standing column, Zib Pharaon, which shows that there were at least the beginnings of a city there in that period. Further, there is evidence that two walls, probably of about this time, enclosed a fairly large area on either side of the valley (see plan on page 110), but this may have been done after peace was made with Antigonus.

Strabo, the only other classical writer who refers to Petra, had his information from one Ahenodorus, the friend and tutor of the Emperor Augustus, who was born there. He describes the Nabataeans and their city as it was in the first century B.C., and the description fits very closely the remains we see today. He says:

The Nabataeans are temperate and industrious, so that a public penalty is imposed on him who lessens his property, but to him that increases it honours are given, and, having few slaves, they are served for the most part by relations or by each other, or they serve themselves, and the custom extends even to the kings. They form "messes" of thirteen men each and two singing girls to each mess. The king in his great house holds many "messes." No one drinks more than eleven cups in one and then another golden beaker. Thus the king is a democratic one, so that in addition to serving himself he sometimes even himself serves others. He often also submits his accounts to the people, and sometimes also the conduct of his life is enquired into. Their dwellings are extensive structures of stone, and their cities are unwalled on account of peace. Most of it abounds in fruit except the olive: they use oil made of sesame. Their sheep are white haired, their oxen large; the country does not produce horses, camels render service instead of them. Even the kings go out without tunics in girdles and slippers, but they go out in purple. . . . They think dead bodies no better than manure; as Heraclitus says, corpses are more to be thrown away than dung heaps. Wherefore they bury even their kings beside their privies. They honour the sun, setting up an altar in the house, making libation on it daily and using frankincense. . . . The capital of the Nabataeans is the so-called Petra, for it lies on ground in general even and level, but guarded all around by rock, outside precipitous and abrupt but inside having abundant springs for drawing water and for gardening.

There are some statements here which do not tally with what now exists, particularly the one about disposal of the dead; the great number of elaborately carved tombs suggests rather a cult of the dead, and if indeed their kings are buried beside their privies these must have been singularly magnificent ones. But the account shows that during the third and second centuries B.C. Petra had gradually been built up into a rich center of the caravan trade from Arabia, and it was very conveniently situated for forwarding of goods to Palestine and the Mediterranean, Egypt and Syria.

The first king of Nabataea mentioned in history is Aretas I, in about the late second century B.C., and to him Jason, high priest in Jerusalem, fled when driven out of his own country. King Obodas I, about 90 B.C., defeated Alexander Jannaeus, ruler of Palestine, in battle, and recovered Moab and Gilead, which Alexander had previously captured. Ammon is not mentioned, but Nabataean pottery of the first century B.C. has been found in tombs there, and so the whole of East Jordan must have been under Nabataean rule at that time. Under Aretas III, son of Obodas, the kingdom was extended to Damascus; he concerned himself much with politics in Palestine, and the Roman Emperor Pompey sent an expedition against Petra under the general Scaurus, but the Nabataeans repeated their tactics with Demetrius and bought him off, thus continuing as an independent nation.

The next king, Malchus II, sided with the Parthians when they made war against Rome, and when they were defeated he had to pay tribute to the Romans (about 40 B.C.). Later Mark Antony gave a large part of Arabia, including Nabataea, to Cleopatra, and the tribute had to be paid to her. Malchus became slack in his payments, and Herod the Great combined with Cleopatra to attack him. Owing to treachery Herod was defeated, but later, in 31 B.C., gained a great victory and took possession of a large part of the country. Malchus was succeeded by Obodas III, who reigned from 28 B.C. to 9 B.C., and during his reign the emperor Augustus planned an expedition against Arabia. Syllaeus, chief minister of Obodas, offered to guide the army through the desert, but proceeded to take them through the worst and most arid parts of it, so that large numbers died of thirst. Obodas conducted great intrigues against Herod with Caesar, as he had wanted to marry Herod's sister Salome and had been refused, but all this had little effect on Petra, whose trade continued to flourish.

Aretas IV, who succeeded Obodas, reigned from 9 B.C. to A.D. 40, and called himself "Rahem ammoh," lover of his people. His reign was prosperous and comparatively peaceful, the only war being one he had with Herod Antipas, son of Herod the Great, who had married his daughter. Herod wanted to divorce her and marry his brother's wife Herodias, and the insult to his family caused Aretas to give battle to and defeat Herod. The Romans, however, backed Herod, and were marching on Petra to avenge him when Emperor Tiberius died and the troops withdrew. Aretas is mentioned in the New Testament, as it was his representative who was governor in Damascus at the time of the imprisonment of St. Paul, who escaped by being let down in a basket through a window. During the reign of Nero (A.D. 67) Malchus III sent troops to help the Romans against the Jews, but hardly anything is known of Petra until the last king, Rabel II, died in A.D. 106, after which the country became a Roman province. The Romans took the city in hand, and redesigned it on the regular Roman model, with a main street of columns and all the usual Roman trimmings. Part of this street has recently been excavated.

The city continued to flourish for some time, and the tomb of one of its Roman governors has an inscription which tells us that in addition to his usual duties he was also responsible for the minting of coins. Nabataean coins were, of course, modelled on the Greek and Roman types, but it is a curious fact that not a single gold Nabataean coin has ever been found and silver ones are extremely rare. Changing trade routes and the rise of the rival city Palmyra in the north caused a gradual decline in the fortunes of Petra, and it was no longer talked about by contemporary historians. But it followed the pattern of history of the rest of the Middle East, and in due course adopted Christianity. An inscription in the great Urn tomb tells us that the interior was converted into a church in the fifth century, and there was a bishopric of Petra. Excavation shows that the street of Columns fell into disuse, and, like that at Jarash, small shops and hovels were built over it. It was still partly occupied when in the seventh century Islam became the dominant power, but soon after it sank into obscurity, and except for the building, in the twelfth century, of a castle by the crusaders which they called Sel—evidently a survival of the early name Sela—it remained in more or less tranquil seclusion until the beginning of the nineteenth century.

The Monuments

Cars have to be left at the police post of Elji, and from there the visitor must proceed either on foot or by horse into Petra itself, although a road is presently being constructed which will eventually enable the visitor to take his car almost up to the entrance of the Syk. The track from the police post leads through the middle of the little village and steeply down into a valley running west. In this valley are seen the first characteristic Nabataean monuments; on the right are two free-standing towerlike tombs, four-sided and about 30 feet high, with the typical crow-step or battlemented design at the top (Plate 16c). A little farther on, on the other side of the valley, is the so-called Obelisk tomb, named from the four obelisks on the upper story. The valley turns to the right, but there is a path which goes straight on up

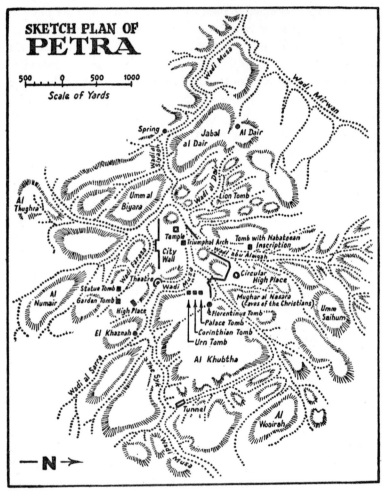

Fig. 6. Plan of Petra

the rocks to the suburb of Petra called Al Madras, which is the ancient Nabataean name as recorded in an inscription. There are monuments of all kinds here as in Petra.

Following the valley to the right, one is suddenly confronted with a great dam, partly collapsed, built of large sandstone blocks, and which seems to prevent further progress, but on the left is a narrow opening or cleft in the cliff face. This is the way into

Petra, called the Syk, and a handful of men could hold it against an army (Plate 14). Soon after entering the cleft there are above the fragmentary remains of a triumphal arch, and the spring of the arch can be seen on either side; this was still standing until as late as about 1896. The road goes straight down the torrent bed, and, as one penetrates farther in, the sheer rock face on either side gets higher and higher, and there is no sound save the clatter of the horses' hoofs on the pebbles and the wind sighing through an occasional oleander bush. Sometimes the rock almost meets overhead, and all is dark and cool; at others it opens out and the scene is flooded in sunshine. On either side can be seen rock-cut channels for bringing the water from Ain Musa into the city; occasionally where the rock has fallen away the channel is made up with blocks of stone. The road goes on and on, seeming endless, but actually for about one mile, the only relief from the enclosing walls being an occasional side valley giving, perhaps, a glimpse of a broken rock-cut stairway leading to some now-forgotten house or place of worship. Originally the whole way had been paved with large blocks of hard limestone, and in some places where the torrent has cut down through the fall of stones and soil these paving blocks can be seen in section. There are small niches carved irregularly in the sides, usually containing the representation of the god Dushara, a rectangular block of stone or an obelisk; these are sometimes single and sometimes in groups.

Just when it begins to seem there can be no way out of this narrow, winding canyon, one is pulled up short by a glimpse straight ahead of part of a magnificent façade adorned with columns and statues. The best time to arrive here is between ten and eleven in the morning, for then one emerges from the gloom of the Syk into brilliant sunshine which lights up the façade of one of the most impressive of all Petra's monuments, El Khaznah. This is a sight which will never be forgotten, for the rock here is really "rose red" and in the sunlight it glows as though it was giving off radiance; the effect is enhanced by the dark green of the oleander bushes in the foreground. Being at a point secluded from wind and rain, the beautiful lines of the architecture are still clear and fresh, though the sculpture has suffered badly at human hands. Like all the large monuments of Petra save one, it is carved from the living rock, and represents a building of two stories, the upper one having a broken pediment on either side and a circular kiosk in the center. This is topped off by a large urn which is badly battered as a result of having been shot at with rifles by numberless people, on account of a tradition that it contains a vast treasure of gold. Hence its name, which means "the treasury." Actually the urn, like the rest of the building, is of solid rock.

There is much discussion among experts as to whether it is temple or tomb, but the weight of evidence seems to point towards the former. The carvings are too damaged to be of much help in identification, though there are some who claim to be able to recognize the goddess Isis in the central figure. The interior consists of one central room with a small room in the back wall approached by three steps, and a small room on either side of the portico. Like all the Petra monuments, it is the façade, not the interior, that was important. It was probably carved in the late second century A.D.

Farther down the valley, some way up on the right, can be seen the continuation of the water channel, which has here been changed into a pipe line, made of short lengths of pottery pipe set in lime plaster. There are numbers of tombs on either side, many with the typical Nabataean crowstep design on them, but it must be emphasized that not every rock-cut cavern is a tomb. Many are dwellings, sometimes of two or three stories, and on some of the cliff faces regular tiers of streets of such houses can be seen. On the left is the theater, capable of seating about 3,000, in the construction of which many early tombs were cut away or sliced through. It is one of the few things which gives us some indication of the relative age of the different types of tomb. The theater was probably cut in the second or third century A.D.

Immediately beyond, the wadi takes a sharp turn west, and runs through the middle of the open area, which is the site of the city itself. The slopes on either side are littered with dressed sandstone blocks, all that remains above ground of the temples, baths and houses of the city. There were at least two bridges across the torrent bed; it may even at one time have been completely vaulted over, but the torrents of the last thousand years have not left much evidence of either. On the south side of the wadi is a stretch of the paved street, which has recently been cleared; the bases of the columns are still largely *in situ* on the south side of the street, but the columns themselves have disappeared except for a few drums re-used in later buildings. On the edge of the torrent bed, where a wall has been constructed on the ancient foundations to try to reduce erosion by the floods, can be seen some rooms which are now below ground level. In these was found a great quantity of the fine painted Nabataean pottery, as well as some Nabataean ostraca or inscriptions on potsherds—even in one case on a complete bowl.

At the end of the excavated part of the street are the ruins of a triple arch, once adorned with carving and sculpture which now lies about in a more or less mutilated condition. The carving, particularly of the floral designs which have survived, is very fine, and typical of the Nabataean type of work. Nearby is a colossal bust and remains of two others, which must have been set up in the façade of some neighboring building now collapsed. The paved road must have continued on through the arch, apparently with some steps, as far as the temple, for there are still a few flagstones to be seen in position just west of the arch. Judging from the type of sculpture, the arch was probably built some time in the first century A.D.

At present it is the temple at the foot of the western cliff which dominates the scene (Plate 16 B); it is called Qasr al Bint, or Qasr Bint Pharaon, the castle of Pharaoh's daughter, from the early Arab habit of ascribing everything of monumental proportions to the all-powerful rulers of ancient Egypt. It is the only built, as opposed to rock-cut, monument still extant, though the precarious state of the walls and the great arch make one wonder how much longer it will remain standing. It would seem to have been erected under Roman domination, perhaps late second or early third century A.D., but nothing whatever is certain about it. In plan it consisted of a portico with two columns between the side walls, then the entrance with the great arch, then another blank area, and finally the back wall divided into three compartments, and the outer two of which seem to have had second stories. The back wall itself is double, with about 3 feet between the two shells, and another peculiar feature of the construction is the use of wooden beams in the walls, perhaps as an anti-earthquake device. Actually these beams, because they have rotted away in the course of time, have been a considerable contributory factor to the collapse of the structure. The whole temple was decorated, at least outside, with carved stucco or plaster, some remains of which can be seen on the outside of the back wall, and with large blocks of stone banded in bright colors.

The hotel camp is usually situated near the temple, and some of the rock-cut dwellings in the eastern cliff are used as bedrooms. A short distance to the south is an unfinished tomb, showing how they were made from the top downwards. On the slopes to the east of the temple is one standing column, sole survivor of another temple; the other columns can be seen lying on the ground with bases, drums and capitals all in order, just as they were thrown down in some earthquake.

All the monuments so far mentioned can be seen without climbing, and there is yet another group involving very little effort to visit them—the monuments in the eastern cliff, which can be seen from the camp. The principal ones are those known as the Urn tomb, the Corinthian tomb, the Palace tomb and the Florentinus tomb, though with the exception of the last there is still argument as to whether they are tombs, temples or dwellings. In view of the nature of the interior, they are most probably tombs, perhaps royal ones.

At a considerably higher level than any of the others is the Urn tomb, a very imposing monument with an open courtyard and colonnades cut in the rock, and an extension of the courtyard was originally built out on an elaborate system of vaults in two stories, now very ruinous. The façade of the tomb is impressive in its simplicity and the great height of the pilasters in comparison with its width. The room inside is 66 feet wide and 59 feet deep, and except for some recesses in the walls is entirely without ornament. The walls and roof are finished off with the characteristic 45-degree Nabataean pick dressing, the corners and angles are as sharp today as when they were first made, and the whole effect is one of cleanness of line and excellence of finish. It is a magnificent example of the unadorned Nabataean stone-dressers' art. On the back wall is a painted inscription in Greek which records that the room was in use as a church in A.D. 447. Above the main entrance is a badly weathered bust, also another chamber; there is no record of this having yet been explored.

Next in order to the north is the Corinthian tomb, very similar in style to the Khaznah, but so badly weathered as to be almost unrecognizable. The doorways are each of different style and size, and lead to different-sized independent rooms, a strange phenomenon for which there is at present no adequate explanation. It is neither a particularly beautiful nor interesting monument, but calls for mention on account of its size and obvious importance in ancient times.

Adjoining to the north is the Palace tomb (Plate 15c), so called because the façade is evidently intended as a copy of a Roman palace of three stories. In this it is unique in Petra, and it is also one of the largest monuments there. With so vast a façade, however, the four doors lead into quite small rooms, of no particular interest. The uppermost story is partly constructed in masonry, as the rock face at this point does not go high enough to accommodate it. On some of the moldings at the extreme right can be seen remains of painted decoration.

About 1000 feet farther on is the tomb of Sextus Florentinus, whose name is given in a Latin inscription above the entrance, of which the following is a translation:

To Lucius . . . minius, son of Lucius Papirius Sextius Florentinus, Triumvir for coining gold and silver, military tribune of Legion I Minerva, Quaestor of the province of Achaia, Tribune of the Plebs, Legate of Legion VIIII Hispania, Proconsul of the province of Narbonensis, Legate of Augustus, Propraetor of the province of Arabia, most dutiful father, in accordance with his own will.

He would appear to have been a gentleman of some importance locally, and the tomb is a very fine one, though not particularly large; the date is about A.D. 140.

These are the chief monuments within easy access, except for a tomb in the Wadi Turkomaniah, which has a long and very interesting inscription in Nabataean over what was once the door. This reads as follows:

This tomb and the large and small rooms within, and the graves fashioned as loculi, and the enclosure in front of the tomb, and the porticoes and the houses within it, and the gardens and the triclinium, the water cisterns, the terrace and the walls and the rest of the entire property which is in these places, is the consecrated and inviolable property of Dushara, the God of our Lord, and his sacred throne (?), and all the gods, (as specified) in deeds relating to consecrated things according to their contents. And it is the order of Dushara and his throne and all the gods that, according to what is in the said deeds relating to consecrated things, it shall be done and not altered. Nor shall anything of all that is in them be withdrawn, nor shall any man be buried in this tomb save him who has in writing a contract to bury according to the said deeds relating to consecrated things, for ever.

The triclinium referred to is a hall in which the funeral feast was held, with benches or couches on three sides, and there are many examples in Petra, though the one pertaining to this particular tomb cannot now be identified. The tomb probably dates from the first century B.C. or A.D.

There are some interesting monuments, tombs, houses, triclinia and Dushara niches in the area of Mughar al Nasara (the Christian quarter), to the north of the Florentinus tomb, and a pleasant and interesting morning or afternoon can be spent discovering and investigating there, and tracing the remains of the rock-cut road which led to the northern suburb of Al Barid. But some of the tombs here are, in due season, inhabited by families from Wadi Musa and their animals, and when they go they leave their fleas behind. These are apt to be rather hungry if the family has been away long.

There are numerous other tombs, houses and sacred places carved in the rock all around, far too numerous for even a passing mention in a work of this size, but perhaps attention should be called to the circular place of sacrifice on the hill opposite the temple to the north, called Arqub al Hishah. There is another sacred place with a triclinium on the hill (Jabal al Maisarah al Sharqiah) opposite Arqub to the west. In the Wadi al Siyagh are some good examples of rock-cut houses, and farther down the same valley to the west is a beautifully situated natural pool, with a small waterfall. An astonishing feature of this valley is the way in which the sheer cliff face has been cut and dressed to a very considerable height; no reason can be seen for this immense labor. Another remarkable feature to be seen here, and by the side of most of the larger rock-cut monuments, is a series of small, shallow rock cuttings, generally in pairs, which go straight up the vertical face of the dressed rock. The purpose of these is wholly obscure. It has been suggested that they were used by the workmen to gain access to the higher parts of the workings, but they seem singularly precarious for such a purpose, and to climb up an absolutely vertical face of rock with no other help than these small cuttings appears well-nigh impossible. At Al Thughra, to the south of the camp site, is an interesting and unique snake monument, with a coiled serpent surmounting a free-standing block of rock, and more early tombs (Plate 16A).

There are two other monuments which should not be missed, with various diversions on the way there; both involve a certain amount of climbing to get to them. These are the temple called Al Dair (the monastery), and the High Place of Sacrifice.

To reach the Dair you cross the Wadi al Siyagh from the camp area and go up the Wadi al Dair. Very soon you reach the remains of the original rock-cut road which led up to the temple, which has steps at steep points of ascent. This road can be followed almost the whole way with only short gaps here and there. Soon after negotiating the first stretch of it, there is in a depression on the left a triclinium with an interesting façade, on which are carved human masks and on either side of the door a lion. A little farther on the track turns left up a wadi, and the ancient road in the form of wide steps is picked up again. On the right (north) from these steps is a side valley, a short distance up which is a kind of grotto with water dripping from the overhanging rock, and many Nabataean inscriptions on the rock face indicate that this was a sacred place. Continuing on up the ancient road, the only other thing of interest before reaching the Dair is the ruins of a Christian hermitage high up on the cliff face on

117

the north of the track, at a point where there is a gap in the ancient road. Some Greek inscriptions and crosses can be seen on the rock, but it is hardly worth the climb up to the place itself.

At first glance the Dair does not appear to be very large (Plate 15B), but in fact it is one of the largest monuments in Petra, and is 165 feet wide and nearly 148 feet high to the top of the Urn; the door is 23½ feet high. Inside, the chamber is, as usual, quite plain, but with a niche in the back wall in which a block of stone representing Dushara was originally left projecting. A few small crosses carved on the wall show that the place was used for worship in Christian times. The ground in front of the temple has been levelled, and there are traces of a stone circle still to be seen, but no other indications of the mode or type of worship carried on there. The Dair was probably carved in about the third century A.D. From a point to the west a wonderful view is obtained across the Wadi Arabah to Palestine and Sinai, while to the south can be seen the high peak of Jabal Harun surmounted by a little shrine covering the traditional site of Aaron's tomb.

To reach the High Place of Sacrifice, perhaps the principal of the Nabataean places of worship in Petra, you start from the camp area by crossing the ridge by the standing column over the ancient rubbish dumps of the city, and up into the Wadi Farasa. A little way up this valley is the monument known as the Tomb of the Roman Soldier, on account of the statue in the central niche over the door (Plate 15A). It is an imposing though small façade, and the chamber has some loculi or graves cut into its walls and arched recesses on the south wall. Opposite this tomb is a very fine triclinium, the interior of which is decorated with engaged Ionic fluted columns; the rock here is also remarkably banded in colors. This was probably the triclinium belonging to the tomb, in which were held the funeral feasts.

Proceeding on up a flight of worn steps, there is on the left a small temple, very much weathered and damaged; above it is a very large water cistern. A short distance farther up the valley the climb commences with a narrow flight of steps running along the cliff face on the east. It is a tricky path to negotiate, yet the local donkeys, loaded, frequently make the journey. It would seem that at some points they must sprout wings or hands to do it!

Arriving at the first platform, there is a large lion carved in the rock opposite; a water channel comes from a cleft above, and in all probability the water originally spouted from the lion's mouth. The animal has suffered badly from weathering and human destructiveness, and is just recognizable. To continue on the way, you can either climb up the water gully above the lion, which is a short cut but not too easy, or there is a perfectly safe, easy way on to the left as you face the lion. The only other things to notice on the way up are some Nabataean inscriptions on a smooth rock face on the left, though they mostly say only "Peace to so-and-so, son of so-and-so."

A great area on the top of the ridge has been quarried away, and two obelisks left standing give some idea as to the quantity of stone removed. Some authorities see a religious significance in these obelisks, and Dushara is always represented by such stand-ing stones, but it is difficult to see how they could have func-tioned in any religious ceremonies. It would have been much easier to have erected a monolith than to cut the rock away all round in order to leave one. On a high point can be seen the remains of a building which probably housed the priests who functioned at the Place of Sacrifice. The place itself occupies a small levelled area just to the north of these buildings, and con-sists of a large triclinium with an altar in the center of its western side, which altar is approached by a flight of three steps. Close beside it to the south is a second altar, which has a circular basin in front of it having a hole in the center leading to a run-off channel, suggesting that here the animal was sacrificed and the blood carried off in the channel. Farther south again is a water cistern. Nothing is known of the ceremonies conducted here, and whatever they were few people could have witnessed them, for there is not room on the platform for very many. This is one of the highest points in Petra, and the view is very impressive. It is possible to return by a different route down a cleft to the east of the High Place, which brings you out at a point near the theater.

These, then, are the chief monuments of Petra. Actually one could spend several weeks in the place and see something new every day. There are, for example, suburbs to the north, called Al Baidha and Al Barid, and one to the south: Al Sabrah. There is the ruined Crusader Castle at Woairah on the east and remains of another on top of Al Habis, the small hill immediately to the west of the Roman temple. There is the alleged tomb of Aaron on top of Jabal Harun, but there is still some local prejudice against strangers visiting the place, and indeed there is little enough to be seen when you have made the arduous climb. Then there are the scanty Iron Age remains on top of Umm al Biyara (the Mother of Cisterns), which is perhaps the most difficult and hazardous climb of all. Practically every hilltop and mountainside has its quota of monuments, but one needs limitless time and enthusiasm—and an expert guide—to see all these. Petra is one of those places which you find either incredibly attractive and beautiful, or depressing and sinister. Most people find it the former, but even so broadminded a traveller as Doughty obviously disliked the place intensely. But whether you like or dislike it, it is something which should be seen, for there is nothing else like it in the world.

Chapter VII

MAAN is the administrative center for the southern district, which is inhabited chiefly by the Bedouin tribes. It is situated on the very fringe of the desert, and from the railway station one can look out east across a vast, apparently empty and flat stretch of country. In fact, it is only the high plateau which is at all flat: the rest is broken and hilly country, called Jabal Tubaiq, which merges gradually with the sandstone district of Hasma to the south. There are still a few tribes who are wholly nomadic, spending their lives in goathair tents and moving from pasture to pasture and water to water. Maan is their shopping center and metropolis, to which they trek with their produce and animals for sale, returning with their other simple necessities of life, all of which can be bought in the markets of Maan.

The town is built almost entirely of sun-dried mud brick, and to the northwest there is an old and almost disused part which is gradually disintegrating and crumbling away. The railway station and aerodrome are at a distance from the town proper to the east, and many visitors for Petra arrive here either by train or air. There is an hotel at the station, where accommodation— a little primitive but adequate—can usually be obtained. The town has nothing of archaeological interest for the visitor, the earliest structure there being the square pilgrimage fort, built about the eighteenth century A.D. The little ruined buildings

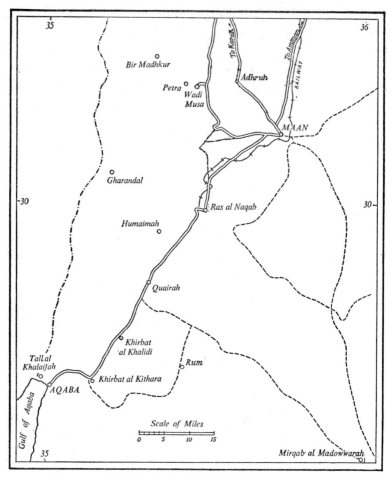

Fig. 7. Map IV showing the Maan and Aqaba regions

which crown a number of hills round about were put up when King Husein of the Hijaz was intending to make his last stand there against the Saudi forces, soon after the First World War. But there is evidence that prehistoric man was here, for in the wadi bed large Palaeolithic hand axes are often found, washed down from some nearby site, for they are not much rolled and abraded by water action.

The road to Petra and Aqaba leads out of Maan to the west,

though the road to Petra is not yet completed all the way. The scenery as far as Ras al Naqab is dull, for the whole area is a monotonous, gently rolling plateau, averaging 4,000 feet above sea level, and bitterly cold at night even in the height of summer. At Ras al Naqab is the railway terminal, to which goods trans-shipped at Aqaba are brought by truck. Soon after leaving Ras al Naqab, a turn in the road suddenly reveals the most startling and beautiful view in the whole of Jordan, for the plateau ends abruptly at a great cliff, which drops steeply down to the plain some 2,000 feet below. This plain is covered with pink sand, and jutting up out of it are hills of sandstone, red, brown and white, eroded into strange, jagged outlines. To the southeast the sandstone mountains of Jabal Rum can be seen, while south-west is the granite end of the Shera range (Mount Seir), which continues down to Aqaba. The whole area down as far as Saudi Arabia is called the Hasma. The view from Ras al Naqab is vast, and quite indescribable, and if you are so fortunate as to come upon it in the early morning or late afternoon when the sun is casting long shadows and there is a hint of mist on the plain, it is a sight which will never be forgotten.

At Ras al Naqab there used to be a ruined Nabataean fort of that name, one of a series which protected the caravan route from Arabia to Petra, but it was used as a stone quarry for road-building operations during the Second World War. Perhaps one should not complain too loudly, for at least the road is fairly smooth and passable in all weathers now, which was certainly not the case before. The road twists and winds its way down a spur, with many hairpin bends and steep slopes, then bounds away across the plain in a straight line. On every side rise the strange sandstone hills, and though they look completely bare of any human traces, there are in many of them rock-cut cisterns, built-up dams, and many of the rock faces are covered with graffiti in Nabataean, Thamudic and occasionally Greek. And to the west of the road, though not visible from it, not far from the foot of the cliff, is the ruin of the little town of Humaimah, where in the eighth century A.D. the Abbassid faction hatched the plots which resulted in the downfall of the Umayyad Caliphate and the transfer of the capital from Damascus to Baghdad (see page 36). About halfway across the plain, to the east of the road, can be seen the desert patrol fort of Quairah, where there used to be a Nabataean fort also. This, too, has disappeared, having been used to provide material for building its modern counterpart; but the great cistern constructed by the Nabataeans is still there and is used to provide water for the men and animals stationed in the fort.

A few miles farther on a track leads off to the east to Rum and Madawwarah, the latter being the most southerly point of Jordan's frontier with Saudi Arabia. The mountains now begin to draw together, and after a few more miles the Wadi Ithm al Jad is entered. For the greater part of the length of this wadi the road has to run down the torrent bed, for the sides are too steep and rough to be able to raise it to a higher level without great expense and many bridges. As a result, it is frequently in a rather sad state of repair and only patches of the surfacing, which was hopefully laid down one summer during the war, have survived the first flood water. The mountains on either side of the deep, narrow gorge are of granite, and are patterned with black and dark green veins, cracks in the mass which in remote geological times filled with lava and volcanic ash.

KHIRBAT AL KHALDI

Not far from the entrance to the valley, and slightly above the road on the east, is Khirbat Khaldi, another of the chain of Nabataean forts protecting the caravan route. These are spaced at what must have been a day's march apart, as were the Turkish forts protecting the pilgrimage route from Damascus to Mecca. This fort has not been plundered for stone, and the walls still stand some 6½ feet high, though the rooms are filled with tumbled debris. The cisterns attached to it were, however, cleared out during the war and pressed into service again; despite the fact that their catchment area was not cleared of the accumulated stones, they almost filled with water each rainy season. They are partly rock cut and partly built, and the roof is made by laying a series of long, thin slabs of stone across arches which spring from the walls of the cistern. In one of them was found a coin of the Byzantine age, suggesting that it was still in use then, but the forts and their cisterns were most probably built in the first century B.C.–A.D.

KHIRBAT AL KITHARA

There is one more such fort at the junction of the Wadi Ithm al Jad with the Ithm al Imran, called Khirbat al Kithara; it is similar in plan and style to the others. The southern route to Wadi Rum runs up the Ithm al Imran, but it is not always passable, as it is very sandy in patches and drifts sometimes form across it. From this junction onwards, the wadi narrows considerably and is littered with huge granite boulders; the mountains rise almost sheer on either side. Just before reaching the mouth of the valley there is an ancient dam across it, much battered by the boulders hurled at it each year by the flood water. There is nothing whatever to indicate the date, but it is probably Roman or Nabataean.

Soon after passing this monument, the road emerges from its narrow confines and in the distance is the Red Sea, shimmering under the sun and unbelievably blue despite its name. The whole setting is one of great beauty, with the mountain masses on the east and west rising out of the ultramarine water, and in the center a flat plain and a narrow, pebbly beach fringed with palm trees.

AQABA

A mere seventeen years ago Aqaba was just a little fishing village, its mud-brick houses nestling among the palm groves, with donkeys in a leisurely way turning the water wheels (one to each garden) to irrigate the vegetables and fruit trees which grow easily, with almost tropical lushness. There is abundance of fresh water at not more than 7 feet below the surface, and a hole dug within 3½ feet of the sea's edge would yield drinkable water. A little desultory fishing was indulged in, not more than was necessary to supply the modest needs of the village, and there was a delightful air of happy indolence about the place which, combined with the warm sun and sea and the cool shade of the palm groves, produced an authentic lotus-eating atmosphere. But already, even then, the modern world was beginning to invade the peace, in the form of an army camp and a small jetty. Now it is a large and flourishing town, Jordan's only outlet to the sea, and most of her imports come in through Aqaba; Amman merchants have their representatives there, and the ease and indolence are gone forever. In addition to the Arab Legion camp, there was until 1956 a large British army camp just outside the town, and the villagers grew rich on the money which poured into the place.

But in thus being once more a center of commercial activity Aqaba is merely repeating its early history, for the earliest remains of which we know so far in the vicinity are those of an important smelting town some 2½ miles to the west of the present town. The site is called Tell al Khalaifah, and is a low mound lying almost halfway across the bay in the middle of the Wadi Arabah. Though the place is now 1¼ miles from the sea, it may have been the site of Solomon's port of Ezion Geber, for it is the only site anywhere near that was definitely occupied in that period. Unhappily it is not now possible to visit it, for it lies almost on the Jordan–Israel truce line. Tell al Khalaifah was excavated in 1937–1938, but the results have not yet been published. At first it was a puzzle as to why such a position should be chosen for a town, for dreadful winds come howling down the Wadi Arabah from the north and the town was right in their path. But when excavation revealed a series of great furnaces for smelting copper on the north side of the town, the reason was obvious, for the winds would provide the necessary draught for these furnaces. The copper was mined at sites in the Wadi Arabah. The history of the town runs from the tenth to the fifth century B.C., when the smelting was apparently given up and a move made to a more comfortable site nearer the present Aqaba to the west. Connections with South Arabia were revealed by the excavations, and its foreign contacts are emphasized by the pottery, which in general is unlike that seen on any other Jordan or Palestinian sites. Jar sealings bearing the name of Qaus-gabr king of Edom were found, and in its latest levels there were many sherds of the beautiful black-and-red Greek ware. With the change of site went a change of name to Elath or Aila, though this name has now been appropriated for a town on the west side of the gulf.

Of the later towns there are now no visible remains: they are hidden under the sand dunes and mounds and covered by the various military camps. Occasionally some piece of evidence comes to light in the form of sherds or carved stones, and piecing all this together it is possible to say that it continued to be a moderately flourishing town up to the time of Islam. The great road of Trajan from Damascus passed through Amman and Petra to Aqaba, from where two roads went west to Egypt and Palestine. Remains of a Christian church have been found, dedicated apparently to St. Theodore and St. Longinus, and there was a bishop of Aqaba at the time of the Muslim invasion, for in A.D. 639 the Caliph Omar stayed with him on one of his tours. The crusaders occupied the place, and under Baldwin I, about A.D. 1116, the fortress on the island of Graye (now known as Jazirat Firaun near the west coast of the Gulf) was built. Exactly when the fort at Aqaba was first constructed it is difficult to say, but the Sultan Nasir, about A.D. 1320, had some hand in it, and an inscription in the gateway mentions Qansuh al Ghuri, last of the Mameluke Sultans, about A.D. 1505. Thereafter Aqaba vanishes from history until the First World War, when it became for a time the headquarters for the Aram armies under King Faisal (Plate 18B).

WADI RUM

A visit to Wadi Rum is not an easy undertaking, but is well worth the effort; it can be approached either by the southern route from the junction of the two Wadi Ithms or by the northern track from near Quairah. The former is a difficult approach, being slightly uphill most of the way and having many sandy patches. The northern route is the more used and the more easily passable, there being comparatively little in the way of sandy patches to cope with. Both tracks run through extraordinarily beautiful country, and the northern one has the advantage of two fairly large mud flats to cross; needless to say they are not an advantage after rain. These smooth, flat expanses of dry mud are a joy to drive over, for the driver can just sit back and relax and gaze his fill of the scenery once he has put the car on the right course. And the scenery is well worth looking at, with the sandstone hills and mountains rising sheer out of the flat plain, and the long vistas down distant valleys to the south (Plate 18A). Again there are many remains of Nabataean and earlier occupation hidden away in rock clefts, and there are numbers of stone cairns, probably graves, dotted about all over the place; so far no indication of their date has been found.

The Wadi Rum itself is the largest and most magnificent of all the valleys in this area, and is strangely beautiful and impressive—even awe-inspiring. Only T. E. Lawrence has succeeded in giving a satisfactory word picture of the remarkable place, in Chapter 70 of *Seven Pillars of Wisdom*, though even his powers of descriptive writing do not really do it justice. As one drives down the track, which keeps to the western side of the valley well away from its sandy bed, one can see occasional groups of paved enclosures near the foot of the hills, which consist of a rough wall of standing stones. The area so enclosed is paved with equally rough stones, none of them dressed at all. At the center of the back wall, and a short distance in front of it, is usually a group of three stones set upright; sometimes there is only one. These enclosures occur either singly or in groups of five or six together, and neither their purpose nor date is known. If you stop your car at almost any point where there are some large boulders near the track, you will probably find a number of Thamudic graffiti scratched on their sides. There are hundreds of these short inscriptions in the Wadi Rum, most of them merely giving the name of the writer and of his father, though some are accompanied by drawings of animals or humans which are often signed, "So-and-so drew this." These strange inscriptions are known to occur from the southern Saudi Arabia to Maan, but very few are found north of that. They were apparently scratched or hammered on the rocks by the camel drivers of the caravans plying between Arabia and possibly Petra, though it is strange that so far not a single text in this script has been found there. The tribe of Thamud, whose name has been applied to these texts, had its center near Madain Salih in Arabia, and were in existence from about the fifth century B.C. to the seventh A.D.; they are mentioned in the Quran. Judging from the thousands of texts already known, it would seem that in those times almost everyone could read and write at least his own name—a degree of literacy which has not yet been equalled. The names show that the writers were Arabs, for many of them are still in use today, and the script belongs to the South Semitic group of alphabets, the only surviving example of which is Ethiopic; the Abyssinians borrowed it from south Arabia. The Nabataean script, and the modern Arabic and Hebrew scripts, belong to the North Semitic group.

By the great massif of Jabal Rum is a desert patrol fort, completely dwarfed by the mass of the mountain behind it, which rises almost sheer for some 1,500 feet and then slopes gently off the summit 500 feet higher. The sandstone rests on a bed of granite, which here is about 60 feet thick; in the next valley to the west, Wadi al Rumman, the bed is 100 feet thick on the east side and entirely non-existent on the west, where the sandstone rises straight out of the valley. It would appear that all these valleys which run roughly north and south are in reality a series of great geological faults, which split and tilted the whole structure to such an extent that while in the Wadi Ithm the mountains are granite, with no capping of sandstone, east of Rum there is only sandstone and no trace of the granite on which it rests. No doubt it was all part of the titanic upheaval which produced, among other things, the Jordan valley and the Dead Sea.

Behind the fort to the west, just at the foot of the mountain, are the ruins of a Nabataean temple, built probably in the first century B.C., which has been partly excavated, and the plan can be seen from the existing remains. It consisted of a square court with rooms around three sides of it, open to the east, from which it was approached by a flight of steps. Engaged columns decorated the walls of the court, which were plastered and painted to represent marble. In the center stood the main altar, and part of a figure of a seated goddess in sandstone was found there. The temple is similar to that of Tannur on a smaller scale. In a side valley to the south is a spring of water, which seeps out between the granite and the sandstone, and on the rock face around it are many worn Nabataean inscriptions, including also a baetyl of some deity, and the little pool below was originally confined within walls. There are many small springs up and down the whole valley, particularly in the bay of Jabal Rum, but this one has the best flow of them all. It was clearly a sacred spot in Nabataean times, not unlike the one on the road to the Dair at Petra. Between this valley and the temple are the remains of a large cistern, and the channel to conduct the water to it can be traced from the spring.

Farther south from the fort, at the entrance to the Wadi Rum, is another spring in the rock face to the west, which has a palm tree growing by it, from which it is named Ain abu Nakhailah, the spring of the small palm. On the level ground immediately below this spring was a small settlement in Neolithic times, and some fine flints have been found on the surface; there are also traces of walls. The inevitable Thamudic inscriptions also crop up everywhere. Just inside the entrance to the valley, and right in its center at both the north and south ends, are some enigmatic structures, which consist of rows, single and double, of very small circles of stones. Those at the south seem to be associated with some kind of built structure, which the 45-degree dressing of the stone blocks tells us is Nabataean. But what purpose these strange features could have served it is difficult to imagine. In many of the valleys to the east of Rum are ruins of Nabataean buildings and dams, but these can only be reached by camel or on foot, for most of the valley beds are sandy and quite impassable for cars.

130

It is an exciting experience to visit Rum, especially for the first time, for it is utterly different from anything else one has ever seen; indeed, the only other place in the world with which it can be compared is the Grand Canyon of Colorado, where the rock formation is the same, but on a much grander scale.

Chapter VIII

UMM AL JAMAL: A NABATAEAN TOWN · CHRISTIAN OC-
CUPATION · ABANDONMENT · THE RUINS · DESERT CAS-
TLES: QASR AL HALLABAT · HAMAM AL SARAH · AL
AZRAQ · QASR AL AMRA · QASR AL KHARANAH · QASR
AL TUBA · AL MUAQQAR · AL MASHATTA · KILWA

THIS remarkable ruined town lies some seven miles east
of Mafraq and 3½ miles north of the Baghdad road. It is situated
on the edge of the flat desert plain, and is the most southerly
of a large group of towns built of black basalt which extends
right up into the Jabal Druze, the largest and chief of which was
Bosra, now in Syria. There is another similar ruined town 15½
miles to the east, called Umm al Quttain, but that has been
badly pillaged for building stone, and not much of it now remains standing (see map on page 39).

UMM AL JAMAL

At the Mafraq crossroads one turns right down the Baghdad
road, and soon a black smear is visible in the plain to the north
which is Umm al Jamal. At a distance of approximately 6½
miles from the crossroads a track goes off to the north straight
to Umm al Jamal which, as you approach it, gives the impression of being a living rather than a dead town, with its towers
and houses still standing in what appears from a distance to be
a good state of repair. The track leads into the town through a
gap in the wall which completely encloses it; the two gates in
this south wall are choked with fallen stones. The entire town

132

is built of black basalt, a volcanic lava stone which covers a large area of country to the north and east known as the Laja. It is found in many grades and qualities, from a very coarse stone full of bubbles which was used anciently for making querns and flour mills, to a very fine-grained stone capable of taking a high polish on its surface. For building purposes an intermediate quality was used which, though very tough, is fairly easily quarried, cut and dressed, and the techniques evolved for utilizing its peculiar qualities are interesting.

The use of wood was eschewed, very often even for doors, which were made of huge slabs of basalt; to make a roof or ceiling over a room the walls were corbelled out, usually in two stages, to the required height, and the remaining area covered with large slabs of stone (Plate 19c). If the gap was too wide to be bridged direct by slabs, then long, thin joists of basalt were cut, laid across the corbels, and the slabs laid on these. The method of dealing with awkward-shaped rooms or corners is complicated and often rather crude. Another method of roofing was to build a series of arches close together and lay slabs across these; this was the method of roofing cisterns particularly. As a result of this exclusive use of basalt for all building purposes, there are some houses with considerable parts of their upper stories still more or less intact. In general plan the houses follow the usual Eastern style of a courtyard with rooms around, and external courtyard stairs to lead to the upper stories. Many houses have stables with mangers, and in some can be seen a little lavatory or wash place constructed in the thickness of the wall just near the door.

Umm al Jamal seems to have been originally a Nabataean town of some importance, lying on the main route from the south to Damascus, and was probably founded some time in the first century B.C. There are no traces of any earlier occupation on the site. It must have been in the nature of a caravan staging post, and the many open spaces within the town were probably intended to accommodate these passing caravans, which may have given rise to its present name, which means "Mother of Camels." There are no wells or springs in the neighborhood, and the entire water supply had to be collected during the rainy season in cisterns, of which every house had at least one, in addition to large public ones, which are still used by the Bedu of the district. Many Nabataean inscriptions have been found in the ruins, but unfortunately none is of any historical importance or tells the name of the town in those days. Outside the walls are a number of large Nabataean family tombs, with stelae recording the names of those buried in them; all had been pillaged in ancient times.

Early in the second century A.D. the Romans took it over along with all the rest of the country, and it may then have been called Thantia, for ancient geographers mention a town of that name which, from their accounts, must have been somewhere in this vicinity. An inscription tells us that the Northwest Gate was built in the time of the Emperor Commodus (A.D. 161–192). There are no other known references to the town, but the bare outline of its history can be deduced from the buildings, the potsherds which are scattered over the surface, and the dedication inscriptions of some of the churches. It continued a quiet and apparently unspectacular existence throughout the Roman period and into the Byzantine, when it seems to have been some sort of religious center, for there are remains of no less than fifteen churches in this small town. Indeed, Christianity came early to Umm al Jamal, for the church of Julianus was built in A.D. 345, and is the earliest dated church so far known. It was abandoned somewhere in the eighth or ninth century A.D.

Scarcely anything remains that can be identified as belonging to the early Nabataean period of the town, though the little building (4 on the plan) has been called the Nabataean temple. The evidence for assigning such a title to it is rather negative, but at least it was something different from the usual house. There is one good monument of the Roman period, the Barracks (number 1), which consists of an open courtyard with two-story buildings around it, and a tower at the southeast corner with machicolations near the top; the one entrance also has this feature above it. In Byzantine times it was converted into a monastery, as the inscription punctuated with crosses around the tower testifies. Another building which probably belongs to the Roman occupation is the Praetorium (number 7) or house of the Roman military governor. This was a building of some pretensions, and the ceiling of the reception room is of finely worked stone with a simple molding. The court had a cloister around three sides of it. The gate built in the time of Commodus (number 11) has already been mentioned.

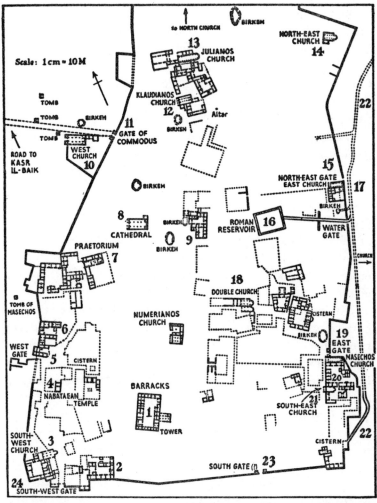

Fig. 8. Plan of Umm al Jamal

The identifiable Byzantine remains are mostly those of churches, though many of the houses may well date from this period also. Only two of these can definitely be dated, that of Julianus and the cathedral, built in A.D. 557. The former (number 13), besides being the earliest, is also the largest church in the town; the latter is quite small (like the cathedral of Jarash) and its dedication is unknown. The Claudianus Church (number 12) is so called because the dedication inscription gives the name of its builder as Claudianus; the same applies to the Church of Masechos (number 19) near the East Gate. No dedication is known for any of the remaining churches; the Southwest Church (number 3), the West Church (number 10), the Northeast Church (number 14, Plate 19B), the East Church (number 17), the Double Church (number 18) and the Southeast Church (number 21).

Among the houses worth noting is the group (number 2), where there are some very fine examples of corbelling so characteristic of the site. In the courtyard of the house (number 6) is a large, well-cut altar, with a fine Nabataean inscription on it. The group of private houses (number 9, Plate 19A) has many features of interest, such as the stables, lavatory and the system of roofing. The building (number 20) has been called the Governor's Palace because it is more spaciously planned than most other houses, and has arched windows in its façade with a small pillar.

Excluding the Water Gate on the east, there are seven gates in the circuit of the walls; two on the west (numbers 5 and 11), two on the east (numbers 15 and 19), two on the south (numbers 23 and 24) and one on the north not shown on the plan. Except for number 11 no dates are known for the building of any of these. Part of the system of water channels for bringing the rainwater into the cisterns can be seen on the east side, just outside the walls (number 22); the water was mostly brought from a small wadi to the north, to the large public reservoir (number 16).

The uncompromising blackness of basalt does not make it a pretty stone to use for building, and it cannot be claimed that

there is much beauty at Umm al Jamal, but it is interesting because of the remarkable state of preservation of buildings which
are now not less than 1,300 or 1,400 years old. So well does the
material stand up to time that at a small village to the east of
Umm al Jamal there are a number of Roman or Byzantine houses
still inhabited by Arab families, and practically unchanged from
the time they were built.

THE DESERT CASTLES

With the exception of Hallabat and Azraq, these castles all
date to the Umayyad period, the eighth century A.D. The Umayyad caliphs were Bedu straight from the Hijaz, Mecca and
Madina, and while they were not unmindful of the comfort and
luxury of their capital Damascus, they seem to have had a
hankering for an occasional retreat into their native desert, but,
having grown out of the idea of living in tents, they caused these
often very elaborate buildings to be set up in various parts of the
deserts of Jordan and Syria. Here they would spend a few weeks
of each year indulging in the desert pastimes of hawking, hunting
and horse racing, and, safe within their desert palaces, the more
sophisticated delights of the Turkish bath, with its attendant
amusements of singing and dancing, were the order of the day,
or more probably night. There are examples of these pleasure
palaces in the desert north of Damascus, but the best are those in
the east Jordan desert and the very fine example at Khirbat al
Mafjar near Jericho. They reveal to the full the voluptuousness of
the Umayyad court, and their love of the arts, particularly painting, sculpture, music and dancing. In these early days of Islam
there seems to have been no objection to the portrayal of human
and animal forms, and the frescoes and carvings with which they
adorned their buildings give a vivid insight into the life of the
period.

Qasr al Hallabat

A few blocks of stone carved with a conventional floral motif
which are found in various parts of the ruin suggest that there

was originally a Nabataean building here, for the style of carving is very similar to that found in the temple at Tannur (Plate 13B), but nothing else of this early phase remains. The main building and outer walls that we see at present date from the Roman period (Plate 20A), and an inscription found some years ago shows that it was erected in the reign of Caracalla, A.D. 198–217. Built into some of the inner walls in the southeast corner and lying about among the tumbled stones are many small basalt blocks bearing parts of what was originally a long inscription in Greek commemorating the rebuilding of the fort under Justinian.

It was one of a series of desert posts put up by the Romans to check and control raiding by the desert tribes. A few miles east of Hallabat is a low wall which runs in a straight line for a distance of about 3 miles across the desert. Although it has semicircular bastions at intervals, it could have served no other purpose than to prevent or break up a charge of nomadic warriors on horseback, and was no doubt part of the general defensive system. Hallabat is situated on an eminence, but the wall is not actually visible from it. The water supply for the fort was kept in a number of cisterns, large and small, in the wadi to the north and west.

Sometime in the seventh century, it became a monastic establishment, and an inscription recording this fact is now built into the main gate of the Arab Legion camp at Zerka. The little building just outside the fort at the southeast corner was a mosque, built probably about the twelfth century A.D. (Plate 20B).

Hamam al Sarah

In the plain some 5 miles east of Hallabat lies the small ruin of an Umayyad hunting lodge and probably a bath, as its name in Arabic suggests; Hamam means "a bath." It is very similar in plan and style to Qasr al Amra near Azraq, but is in a sadly ruined state. Only an occasional small patch of color on the plaster indicates that the walls were once covered with frescoes, again like Amra. Its most interesting feature is the ribbed dome over the entrance hall.

Al Azraq

This little oasis, some 50 miles east of Amman, is interestingly situated on the very edge of the lava country which stretches north and east, and also at the head of the Wadi Sirhan, that great shallow valley which cuts its way down into the forbidden territory of Saudi Arabia, and lures on the mind to follow its so little-known course. Azraq is a typical oasis, with many groves of palms and large stretches of swampy water on which, in season, thousands of duck and other migrating waterfowl congregate to rest during their long journey; many of them fall victims to the guns of ardent hunters.

There is a desert patrol post here, and of recent years there has been much activity on the part of the American Point 4 organization, who have put in hand a plan for draining some of the swamps and canalizing the water to irrigate a large tract of land a little farther south. During the course of this operation they chanced upon one of the most astonishing prehistoric sites yet seen in the country. A spring to the south of the Police post had become blocked by falls of earth and the growth of small bushes, so it was decided to enlarge the area and try to increase the flow. A space about 16 feet square was laid out and work commenced, and about 3 feet below ground level a few fine Palaeolithic hand axes were discovered. The quantity increased as the work got deeper, until finally when it was about 2 feet below water level hand axes were found by the bucketful. In all some 400 of these fine tools were recovered, beside several hundred flakes and other types of implements. Unfortunately the work was not, of course, controlled stratigraphically, so that all that can be said at present is that here is a Palaeolithic site of extraordinary interest and importance, for in no other place has such a quantity of implements of this period been found. These artifacts are nearly all of the lower Palaeolithic period, about 200,000 years ago, but a controlled excavation at the site is necessary to solve the many problems involved, and it has not yet been possible to carry this out.

Winding their way through many of the pools and lakes are a series of ancient walls, which would seem to have had something to do with controlling the water flow, but how they functioned and when they were built cannot now be determined. Just above the palm groves to the north is a fairly large castle built of black basalt (Plate 12A). The date of its foundation is not known, but it certainly underwent several changes in the course of its existence; of this, the earliest evidence is the Greek and Latin inscription on an altar, two fragments of which lie in the courtyard. This tells us that the building was dedicated to the Emperors Diocletian and Maximian, which would probably be about A.D. 300: there is also an inscription of the Emperor Jovian (A.D. 363), who may have enlarged or restored it. It was still in use as a fort at the time of the Muslim invasion, but the next datable evidence is the Arabic inscription over the main door, which records that Azz al Din Aybak built (or perhaps rebuilt) the fort. Aybak was governor of the country from about A.D. 1213 to 1238, during the time of the crusades. Nothing else is known of its history until the First World War, when Colonel T. E. Lawrence had his headquarters here during the latter part of his campaigns, and from here he set out for the final assault on the Turks. The room immediately above the gate was his reception and council room, though nowadays nothing but evil-smelling litter is to be found in it.

Qasr al Amra

This beautiful building (Plate 12B) was constructed between A.D. 705 and 715, during the reign of the Caliph Walid I. It seems to have served the double purpose of hunting lodge and baths, and every available inch of wall inside was covered with very fine frescoes. It is the best-preserved monument of its kind and period known. The actual structure of the building suffered but very little damage from either time or man. Its remote situation may have something to do with this, though even great inaccessibility has not saved Qasr Tuba, another building of the same period.

The frescoes, unfortunately, have suffered much from smoke,

dirt, time and people scrawling and scratching their names all over the place, but are none the less in quite a good state in many parts. Dalton in his *History of Byzantine Art* says of them: "No such extensive decoration in fresco is known to have survived in

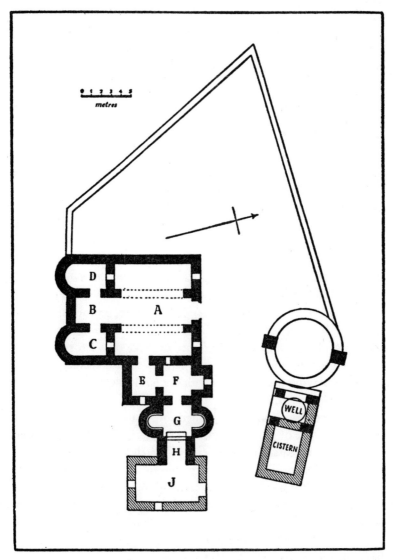

Fig. 9. Plan of Qasr al Amra

any other secular building earlier than the Romanesque period." Some of the rooms have mosaic floors, but these are buried under a large accumulation of rubbish, and the clearing of them and cleaning of the frescoes cannot possibly be undertaken until at the same time they can be adequately protected from further damage of any kind.

The entrance faces north, and leads straight into the great hall (A on the plan, figure 9), which is roofed with three vaults supported on arches. The frescoes on the left hand, east, wall are almost indistinguishable, but consisted of hunting scenes, with figures of Poetry, History and Philosophy on the bay at the south end. Near the north corner of this wall a close examination will reveal a pack of Saluki hunting dogs in full cry. Some shadowy figures and one good head can be distinguished in the south bay. On the right, west, wall is a scene of a lady bathing (?) and some kind of domestic or athletic activity. At the southern end of this wall was a picture of the six enemies of Islam with their names in Greek and Kufic, namely, the Byzantine emperor, Roderick last king of the Spanish Visigoths, Chosroes emperor of Persia, the Negus of Abyssinia, and two others whose names cannot be distinguished. Roderick came to the throne in A.D. 710 and was killed in battle the following year, which sets a very close date for at least this part of the frescoes. This picture, unfortunately, is in a very bad state of preservation. Adjoining these figures on the west bay of the south wall is a figure of Nike or Victory. On the base of each of the great arches can be seen a dancing girl, a musician playing a stringed instrument, and other rather obscure figures (Plate 21B).

The vaulted ceilings are divided into square panels, and each contains a scene of domestic activity; a potter at work, a carpenter sawing logs, a peasant digging, etc. In the alcove B and the rooms C and D the light is too bad to be able to see much, but the side walls of B were painted to represent drapery between columns, and on the back wall was a picture of the enthroned caliph with a Kufic inscription on either side. The walls and ceilings of C and D were decorated with conventional floral motifs, and these rooms have mosaic floors.

Room E contains some well-preserved paintings. The vaulted ceiling is again divided into panels, each containing a picture of some animal, bird or a human being, with naturalistic flowers and trees. Over the door leading from A is a reclining female figure and a very plump winged Eros apparently luring on the lady to something now obliterated. On the left of the window is a seated lady of strange but ample proportions, and on the right is a gentleman also seated, his back to the spectator; the two gaze at each other across the dividing window with sad longing. There is a low bench along the east wall, and this room was the frigidarium or cool room of the baths.

The ceiling of room F has more pictures of animals, birds and humans, and the walls above the cornice are decorated with a highly conventionalized grapevine. Over the door from room E are more well-fed females, one of whom appears to be carrying a bucket or basket. Over the door to G is a tableau featuring similar ladies, and a child (?).

Room G was the caldarium, or hot room, and the furnaces were in the passage H; there were benches in each of the alcoves on the north and south. It has one of the most interesting ceilings, for in the dome is a representation of part of the night sky with the various constellations in their zodiacal houses. It represents one of the earliest attempts to portray a map of the heavens on a dome, and has resulted in some strange errors and misplacements of constellations. Owing to this no close calculation of the date can be made, but it is agreed that it must be between A.D. 500 and 1000. Beyond is room J, which has its entrance outside and was apparently never completed. To the north is the cistern and well, with remains of two pillars which supported the water-raising apparatus: the well is now filled with debris. There are also remains of a circular structure to the west of the well, perhaps another cistern, and from it an enclosure wall runs west, then turns at an obtuse angle and joins the southwest corner of the building, thus forming a large open courtyard.

Qasr Amra is situated in the Wadi Butm, so called from the name of the Butm or Terebinth trees which grow there, making pleasant little patches of green shade in the surrounding aridity.

143

In spring large pools of water remain in the wadi bed, and the place is a favorite haunt of gazelles and many other forms of wild life.

Qasr al Kharanah

This is the only desert castle in Jordan which seems to have been built with a defensive purpose in mind. In appearance it is an imposing, foursquare fortress, with a round tower at each corner and a half-round one between, the high walls pierced below the band of herringbone decoration of bricks by arrow slits, and above by small windows (Plate 22). The only entrance is on the south, flanked by quarter-round projections, and with a large window and a row of decorative niches above. There is still some difference of opinion as to the date of this castle, some authorities considering it to be pre-Muslim, but there is a painted Kufic inscription over the door of an upper-story room on the west which has the date of 92 A.H. (Anno Hajirah, dating from the year of the prophet's flight from Mecca to Madina), which equals September A.D. 711.

In the window over the entrance can be seen the beam of wood forming the lintel. If a piece of this could be submitted to the carbon 14 test it might help to solve the problem of the date of construction. Built into the jambs of the entrance door are two blocks of stone bearing remains of an inscription in Greek, suggesting that there was a building on the site or somewhere in the vicinity in late Roman or Byzantine times. Its commanding position on the scarp of the wadi to the south and at a point where meet many tracks from all directions, including the Wadi Sirhan, makes the site a strategic one.

The doorway leads into the entrance passage, on either side of which are long, arched and vaulted rooms, which were the stables. Next one comes to the open courtyard, on both sides of which flights of stairs lead to the upper story. Originally there were eight square pillars around the courtyard, supporting a balcony on the upper floor. The plan of the ground floor is a very simple one, being just one large room on each of the east, west and north

144

sides, flanked by smaller rooms; these ground-floor rooms are plain and unadorned. The upper story repeats the plan of the ground floor, except on the south, where the area occupied by each stable has been divided up into five rooms. All the rooms are arched and vaulted in some way, and in the larger rooms the springs of the arches are supported on groups of three engaged columns (Plate 22B). The very hard plaster used was frequently carved into decorative patterns, particularly over arches, squinches, etc. Some of the rooms end in semi-domes, with decorated squinches set across the corners. A few of the rooms have medallions of carved plaster or stucco as an ornament, sometimes set loose in stone frames. Over the north door of the large room on the west is the Kufic inscription already referred to, and traces of many others (in addition to scratched tribal marks, etc.) can be faintly seen painted on walls and columns.

The method of constructing arches and vaults is very characteristic, that is, of thin slabs of stone set on edge at a slight angle to each other and held together by an almost equal quantity of hard mortar. The technique is very clear in rooms where the plaster has peeled off the ceiling. This technique is identical with that used in the great castle of Ukhaidar in Iraq, about which similar differences of opinion as to its date exist.

Except for the northwest corner, where an earthquake has caused a huge crack in the wall from top to bottom, the building is in a remarkably good state of preservation. One curious feature of the site is that there seems to be no provision for a supply of water, neither well nor cistern. Pools in the wadi would only provide temporary relief in the spring, and a building of the size of this one, accommodating both horses and men, would have needed more than this. That there is water somewhere in the vicinity is strongly suggested by the following episode. Some years ago, when I visited Kharanah in early summer, a small white dog was noticed wandering about the site and obviously at home, though there were no human inhabitants within miles of the place. Two months later, another person visiting it also saw the same small white dog still living there, and, after all, dogs must drink.

Apparently the dog had succeeded in solving the problem which still defeats us: where the inhabitants of Kharanah got their water.

About a mile west-southwest of the castle, in the bed of the wadi, is a magnificent Upper Palaeolithic-Mesolithic site, where the ground is covered with thousands of flint implements and flakes. The exact place is, however, difficult to find, as natural flint also abounds in the neighborhood.

Qasr al Tuba

Some 29 miles almost due south of Kharanah is another Umayyad castle called Qasr al Tuba: it is the most southerly and remote of all the desert castles. That it is Umayyad is clear from the style of the carved stonework, but it is the only clue as to its date. It is entirely different from any of the other castles, being built partly of stone and mud brick. It is also, with the exception of Mafjar in the Jordan valley, the largest of them all, or was intended to be, for it was never finished (Plate 23). It was planned as two identical halves, but most of the southern half never got beyond the foundation stage. In the northern half are some fine, large rooms with high vaults of mud brick, but despite its remoteness the castle is in ruins. Originally there were some beautifully carved stone door jambs and lintels, but these have been mostly smashed or carried away. A good example of a lintel can be seen in the Amman museum.

Al Muaqqar

About 22 miles west of Kharanah, on the Amman track, is the little settlement and desert patrol post of Al Muaqqar, where are the remains of yet another Umayyad castle. This is very ruined indeed, so that even the plan cannot now be satisfactorily ascertained. It was, however, elaborately decorated, for many fine carved capitals, rather in the Byzantine style, have been found on the site. A few years ago, when one of the large cisterns to the east was being cleared out, a column and its capital were found, and the latter has a fine Kufic inscription on one side which dates the building—at least of the cistern—to the Caliph AbdAllah

Yazid, A.D. 720–724. The drums of the column are also inscribed at regular intervals with a scale of measurements in Kufic, the final measure being on the capital which is 15 dhra (forearm) or about 33 feet high. Column and capital must have stood in the center of the cistern to show how much water was there: 33 feet would be a considerable depth.

Al Mashatta

This castle lies some 6 miles southwest of Muaqqar. To get to it from Amman one takes the Maan road, forks left at the junction at Yadudah on to the desert track to Maan, and turns left at the first village of Tanaib (see map II on page 39).

Again there is some uncertainty as to its date, and there are no inscriptions of any kind to give a lead, but most authorities agree that on stylistic grounds it must belong to the Umayyad period, somewhere in the eighth century A.D. It was never completed. The whole façade was originally covered with elaborate and detailed carving, but just before the First World War the Sultan Abd al Hamid of Turkey made a present of the place to the Kaiser, and the sculpture was stripped off and removed to Berlin, where it was set up in one of the museums. A few pieces still remain *in situ* and can also be seen lying about near the entrance gate; these give some idea of the intricacy of the patterns and the indifferent quality of the work (Plate 24A).

The whole complex consists of a great square enclosure, which is divided into three parallelograms; the two side ones extend along the entire length of the enclosure, and the center one has been divided up into three sections. The first of these, nearest the gate, contains the foundations of rooms, the second was an open court-yard and the northern one is entirely occupied by the residence. The principal feature of this is the great hall, trefoil in plan, and approached through a triple archway; the voussoirs or curved stones of the arches are lying in order on the ground as they fell. There was a large dome of burnt brick over the trefoil part of the hall, and all the other rooms are vaulted with burnt bricks. This use of burnt brick as a building material is very unusual in this style of building, and has given rise to many speculations as to the origin of the builders of the palace. Qasr al Tuba is built of sundried, not burnt, bricks.

In the eastern and western sections of the enclosure there is evidence that it was intended to construct more rooms down its whole length, as many stones have been left projecting from the enclosure wall ready for bonding in the cross walls. There are no visible wells or sources of water supply on the spot, but there may well be some buried underground cisterns. The small quantity of debris, stone or bricks within the enclosure is clear evidence that only a fraction of the place was ever completed. Also the carving on the façade was finished only in patches. Unfortunately the place has suffered much from the depredations of people in search of dressed stones for building the nearby station and village of Jiza.

KILWA

One other site in the eastern desert must be mentioned, though it is unlikely that many visitors will be able to get there, for it lies in the heart of the inaccessible Jabal Tubaiq, southeast of Maan. This is Kilwa, some 115 miles from Maan, and without a guide it would be almost impossible to get there by car, for although tracks are shown on the special track map of the country, these vary considerably from time to time, as they are partly obliterated by drifting sand or washed out by flood waters. From Maan the track runs out through Jafar, where is the foursquare castle of Shaikh Auda abu Tayi, famous ally of Colonel Lawrence in the First World War. After Jafar long stretches of mud flats are crossed, almost as flat and smooth as a bowling green, and then the difficult terrain begins, with sand drifts and rough wadi crossings to negotiate. But the scenery is fantastic, with sudden vistas of great plains surrounded by mountains whose sides are covered in slopes of bright red sand. Occasional stunted trees emphasize the general bareness of the country, and one has a real sense of being away from the world.

In the midst of this wilderness, some time probably in the sixth century A.D., a group of monks decided to settle. They built a

148

small village, placed a huge dam across the flat wadi to conserve the meager rains for summer use, and presumably felt they were free from the trammels and temptations of contemporary civilization. What they lived on is something of a puzzle, for it seems unlikely that the water stored by the dam would be sufficient for irrigation and the growing of crops and vegetables, even if the soil were suitable for such a purpose. An Arabic inscription on the lintel of one of the doors shows that the place was still functioning at least in the eighth century A.D., but there is no sign of any later occupation. Despite the centuries intervening, a large expanse of water still collects by the dam in a good year, and the place then becomes the temporary center for a number of Bedu families and their flocks and camels.

But the monks were not the first inhabitants, for on an isolated rock outcrop a few hundred yards northeast of the settlement are scratched a number of drawings of animals and some humans. These date to the Upper Palaeolithic period, some 12,000 or more years ago, and are the only prehistoric drawings so far found in Jordan. They represent the various animals then in existence, chiefly a wild bull and the ibex, and the one group which seems to include humans is difficult to disentangle. Scratched on top of some of the prehistoric drawings are Thamudic inscriptions, which, although made at least 1,300 years ago, are still white and fresh looking, whereas the earlier drawings are patinated a dark brown like the surface of the rock—a good indication of their very early date. Around the base of the outcrop can be found a quantity of flint flakes and implements, presumably contemporary with the drawings.

Chapter IX

THE TOWN of Jericho has great individuality and charm, and is quite different, both in its aspect and its inhabitants, from any of the hill towns. It lies nearly 800 feet below sea level, and is in consequence an ideal winter resort, for often when the hills of Jerusalem and Amman are covered in snow one can bask in hot sunshine in Jericho or on the shores of the Dead Sea. The principal building material used is sun-dried mud brick, and most of the houses have the characteristic pent roofs made of mud and chopped straw mixed, laid on a bed of reeds; this roofing is, when kept in good condition, waterproof. The present inhabitants are largely the descendants of people left behind from the army of Ibrahim Pasha in the early nineteenth century, and include a great number of Negroes and Negroid types. They are charming, friendly and hospitable people, though mostly terribly poor at the present time. They have an inherent love of singing and dancing due, no doubt, at least partly to their Negro ancestry. There are two large camps to the north and south of the town in which are housed many thousands of Palestine refugees, who add a rather unstable and dissatisfied element to the population. They are also one of the causes of the local inhabitants' poverty, for, being fed, housed and clothed by the United Nations, they will work for pocket money of a few shillings a day, and in order to compete with this the locals have to accept the same wage on which, however, they have to subsist entirely.

The place is rich in orange and banana groves, irrigated from the seemingly endless flow of the so-called Elisha's Fountain, a great spring to the northwest of the town. It is a veritable oasis in an otherwise barren area, and it is easy to see why it attracted settlers from the very earliest times.

Ancient Jericho is a small mound called Tell al Sultan, lying beside the spring just referred to, and can have been no more than a village by modern standards, for the area of the mound is very small. Excavations were first started there in 1911 by a German expedition, but they were not very successful. The British School of Archaeology in Jerusalem under Professor Garstang reopened the work in the 1930s and in a series of trenches penetrated to some of the earliest levels of the site, down to the Neolithic of about 6000 B.C., in addition to finding some very fine tombs of the Middle Bronze, Hyksos, period. In 1951 the school again returned to the charge, this time under the direction of Dr. Kathleen Kenyon, and her work has produced some sensational results, especially in the very earliest Neolithic levels of about 7000 B.C.

The mound is an entirely artificial one, and has some 50-foot depth of stratified town levels. As a result of the most recent excavations, when the whole depth was cleared, layer by layer, in a series of trenches to bedrock, the history of the place is now fairly well established, and some unique monuments were uncovered in the process. Originally the mound must have been more than 50 feet high, but the upper levels have been considerably eroded and were also dug away in Roman and Byzantine times for the making of mud bricks. Trench I and its two adjoining squares on the west offer the visitor the best vantage point from which to see the principal discoveries. The vertical face of the trench shows in section the history of the town from the topmost wall of about 1700 B.C., to the earliest remains on bedrock of about 7000 B.C.

Neolithic

The earliest settlement covering the area of the whole mound was of the Neolithic period, and although only a very small area of this has been excavated, it has entirely revolutionized our ideas of early Neolithic man. For the village was surrounded by a great stone wall with a ditch in front of it which can be seen at the very bottom of the trench, and behind the wall is a huge circular tower built of stone and mud, which has a sloping shaft piercing the center of it from top to bottom in which are well-built steps with the treads of hammer-dressed stones. From the foot of the steps a short passage leads out of the tower, and both stairway and passage are roofed with large flat slabs of stone.

These two monuments alone tell two new facts: first, that man in this remote period, about 7000 B.C., was already leading a fully communal life and was prepared to work in conjunction with his fellow men—obviously under a leader or leaders—for the common good, the common good in this case being the protecting of their village from attack by erecting a stone wall all around it, cutting a ditch in the rock and building a tower or possibly towers. The second is revealed in this tower, which shows that already a considerable degree of architectural skill had been acquired, and that a building plan could be drawn up, at least in a person's mind, for without some plan to work to so many things could, and almost certainly would, have gone wrong. These achievements become even more astonishing when one remembers that metal was unknown and only flint and stone implements were available for use. The ditch must have been excavated largely by pounding, and the roofing blocks for the stairway and passage and the stairtreads have been carefully selected from a type of rock that has a natural cleavage of the sort required, and then hammer or pounder dressed.

Not even pottery had been invented in this early period, though unbaked clay was used for making rough figurines, both human and animal. Very fine implements and tools of bone were, however, being used, and soft, colored stones were being carved in rough representations of human and other, unidentifiable, objects. Flint implements include knives, borers, scrapers, arrowheads and sickle blades; the latter suggest that agriculture was already practiced, and there is further evidence for this in the number of querns of conglomerate stone for grinding corn which have been found. Other kinds of stone, not flint, tools have been found, such as hammerstones, grinders, pestles and polishers.

Their architectural ability was not confined to the building of town walls and towers. The private houses were well designed, in the typical Eastern style of rooms around a courtyard, strongly built of handmade mud bricks and with clay floors which were usually coated with lime plaster, the final layer of which was very fine, sometimes red or cream, and finished off by burnishing to a high polish. They had one refinement which has been re-introduced in some modern buildings; the junction of floor and wall was slightly concave, making cleaning easy and lessening the accumulation of dust. Woven and plaited mats were often used on the floors, and the roof must have been similar to those of Jericho houses today, for many pieces of mud with reed impressions have been found.

They had, too, a sense of religion, or at least of the supernatural, for in one room the end wall had a niche in which a chipped, oval stone stood upright in a stone pedestal, the earliest example so far known of the "god stone" or baetyl. Another building of exceptionally large size may have been a temple, though it has not been completely excavated, so this is not certain. The artistic instinct is not lacking either, and a most remarkable achievement in this field is a group of seven skulls, on the actual bones of which, when they had been dried off, the face was modelled in plaster, the features painted and the eyes of inlaid shells divided in the center to give the impression of pupils. The modelling of one of these skulls—the only one with the lower jaw still in position—is of astonishing delicacy, and shows careful anatomical observation (Plate 26B). One can only guess at what purpose these strange objects served; they may have been heads of enemies slain in battle or those of venerated ancestors kept in the house as blessings. But they were much concerned with skulls and with skeletons in general, for groups of skulls have been found carefully arranged together in rooms, and of the numerous skeletons lying around nearly all are disturbed in one way or another.

The town wall referred to was rebuilt three times at three different levels, and these can all be seen in Trench I. These changes of level imply that inside the walls occupation levels were gradually rising—in other words, the mound was beginning to be formed. The early, pre-pottery Neolithic people lived for many centuries at Jericho, and the ruins of their many building levels made a mound some 35 feet high. They were succeeded by a people who, though still in the Neolithic stage, had invented pottery; they would seem to have been invaders from outside, but whether they destroyed the pre-pottery town or found it already deserted must remain in doubt at present. The possession of pottery was the only advance they had made on the earlier people, and in all other ways their culture was inferior. They were probably nomads, for they lived for some time on the mound without building any houses, presumably in tents, and at no time did they build substantial structures. Their village was unenclosed, and nothing resembling a public building has yet been found from this period, and in general their houses were of poorer quality than those of their predecessors. Their tools and weapons were still of flint—sickles, knives, chisels and so on—but such objects are relatively scarce and, owing to the habit of digging into the earlier levels, thereby bringing up objects from these levels, it is often difficult to say to which of the periods the objects belong.

There is also an almost complete absence of burials, skeletons and skulls, so we do not know anything of the physical characteristics of these people. They had their art and religion, which were combined in a find of the remains of three almost life-size statues in plaster, of which, however, only one head remains intact. The technique is not unlike that employed by the earlier people in modelling on the skulls,* but there are significant dif-

---

* Dr. Kenyon informs me that she is now inclined to believe that these statues are in fact pre-pottery Neolithic in date, and that the plastered skulls belong to the end of the pre-pottery period and might stylistically be later than the statue head.

ferences. The head is merely a flat oval disk about an inch thick on which the features are rather roughly modelled, and all the details, such as hair, filled in with painting. Shells are again used for the eyes, but whole shells, not as in the case of the earlier heads divided shells, so there is no appearance of pupils. The group consisted of a trinity—man, woman and child—which suggests that it was a religious group. The early pottery is decorated with red paint in bands, chevrons and lines, and the later type has raised bands of incised herringbone decoration. It is this pottery which is important, for it enables us to link its makers with inhabitants of other parts of the Middle East, as far afield as Syria and Iraq.

Bronze Age

At the end of the Neolithic period, which was about 4000 B.C., there was a gap in the occupation of Jericho, and the site was abandoned for some time. This is shown by two separate pieces of evidence: the accumulation of a layer of humus over the mound which can be identified in the section, and the absence of any remains of the succeeding culture, called the Chalcolithic, when the use of metal was first introduced. The next occupation on the mound can be dated to about 3200 B.C., but for this the best evidence comes from tombs, for from now on the cemeteries supplement the evidence of the town levels and also supply complete examples of objects of which only fragments are found in the houses. The main cemeteries of ancient Jericho are under the refugee village to the north, and tombs have been excavated in the streets and courtyards there.

A most remarkable tomb of this period, for which a carbon 14 test gives a date of 3260 B.C. plus or minus 110 years, contained 113 skulls arranged round the edge of the tomb chamber, in the center of which was a cremation pile of burnt bones; some of the skulls showed signs of scorching, but they had not been deliberately burnt. This implies some very curious burial customs, for it means that the bodies had first been exposed until the flesh disintegrated and the bones separated, then this great group of skeletons was collected, the skulls arranged round the tomb chamber facing inwards, the bones piled in the center with the necessary firing material and set alight. When the pile had cooled off, the funerary offerings, mostly pottery, were placed in the tomb, and the cremated bones covered with a layer of stone chippings. Such customs have not yet been attested from other sites in Palestine or Jordan, though the custom of exposing the bodies until they disintegrated and then burying the bones is not uncommon. Whoever these people were, they were again nomadic in origin. But they were also the forerunners of the succeeding period, the Early Bronze Age, which was one of the most flourishing in the history of Jordan and Palestine.

This Early Bronze Age, running from about 2900 to 2300 B.C., is well represented at Jericho, particularly in so far as the defenses of the town are concerned, and these must have been truly remarkable. In Trench I can be seen in section many of the town walls of the period (Plate 25A), all built in mud brick, and even the topmost one right on the surface is no later than this; all later levels have eroded away. In sites E.III and E.IV can be seen the remains of houses of this period. The defense walls were altered and rebuilt about sixteen times during the course of the 600 years of the Early Bronze Age, and it is often very difficult to disentangle the different periods of rebuilding; walls collapsed, due to earthquakes and undermining by water, and were patched together again. But some of the destruction was due to enemy action, and in Trench III, at the south end of the mound, a dramatic example of this can be seen in section. The wall here was very strong, 15 feet thick, and still stands 11½ feet high; but a tremendous fire was lighted against it, of which the ash can be seen spreading some 24 feet out from the face of the wall and about 3 feet thick. To produce such a depth of ash many tons of brushwood would be needed, and the heat generated was so great that the bricks were burnt red right through to the center of the wall. A constructional feature actually helped the fire, for the builders inserted transverse and longitudinal beams of wood in the wall, no doubt as a strengthener against earthquake collapse, but the beams caught fire and helped in the burning of the wall. Every defense wall of the period, however, shows sign of damage and destruction of some kind and continual rebuilding and patch-ing, and this suggests that the inhabitants of the town then must have lived a very insecure and uncertain existence.

Despite this the general picture shows a steady improvement of culture, with copper being used in considerable quantities for tools and weapons, and the pottery gives evidence of trade with all the surrounding countries. It was a great period of urban growth, with new towns springing up in many previously uninhabited sites. But, like the preceding cultures, it was brought to an end by a nomadic invasion. It would seem that towards the end of this time the Early Bronze Age people began to feel more secure and became careless of their defenses; at some time they received a rude shock in a threatened invasion, and the last wall of the period is hastily botched up on top of the remains of an earlier wall. Loose stone foundations were hurriedly laid and a brick wall begun on top of them; this included pieces of bricks taken from other walls. But before they had time to finish the job disaster was upon them, the wall was destroyed by fire, and the town fell to the invading nomads. The Early Bronze Age in Jericho was at an end.

For a time the newcomers camped on the mound, and later built themselves some very flimsy houses, which spread right down the slopes, as there was no defense wall in this period. One building on the west may have been a temple, for there was an altarlike structure in it and an infant sacrifice beneath its foundations. The most remarkable things these people left behind them were, however, their tombs: in contrast to the multiple burials of earlier ages, each tomb contained one body only, and very few grave offerings. Out of 360 tombs excavated, 248 were of this period, which is known as the intermediate Early Bronze-Middle Bronze period.

Some of these tombs were enormous, with shafts 10 feet wide by 16 feet deep, and a burial chamber 11½ feet by 10½ feet by 7½ feet high, involving the excavation of some 150 tons of rock; all for the burial of one person. The bodies were exposed and the loose bones collected for burial as before. Grave goods vary with the different types of tomb, some having only a single dagger, some pins and beads (presumably for women); others have only a few pots, still others have some pots and a dagger or lancehead. Every one has, however, one common factor: a small niche cut in the wall of the tomb chamber and containing a four-spouted lamp typical of the period. On the smooth rock face of one of the tomb shafts someone had scratched some little drawings of goats or ibex, trees, and two men armed with spears and carrying shields; this is so far the only known example of the art of these people. Their pottery is dull, the only decoration is combed bands and wavy lines, with no color or polish of any kind—strictly utilitarian.

These nomadic people were most probably the Amorites who, between about 2300 and 1900 B.C., overran most of the Middle East, including Mesopotamia and Egypt. They in turn were subdued by another invasion, but of a very different kind from theirs. This time the invaders brought with them a much higher culture than had hitherto been seen in Palestine, chief evidence of which is their pottery. The forms are all new, often very delicate, and all are made on a potter's wheel, whereas up to this time pottery in Palestine had been handmade with sometimes the neck and rim turned on a slow wheel. Their well designed and built houses must have covered the whole of the mound, though it is only on the eastern slopes that they now survive: some can be seen in section in sites H.I–V.

There is some evidence that in the early days of the period, called the Middle Bronze Age, the town was protected by a brick wall as before, but at a later state an entirely new system of defense was introduced, not only in Jericho but all over Palestine. This consists of a steeply sloping scarp of tipped soil faced with plaster and surmounted by a brick wall. There are three of these massive defenses, which were built at different times, all of which can be seen in section in Trench I. The first is nearest the center of the mound, and the sloping layer of white plaster can be clearly traced, with tongues of plaster running in as the different layers of soil were thrown in. The whole of this particular defense can be reconstructed from finds in other parts of the mound, and when complete it consisted of a stone revetment 11½ feet high, a plastered slope at an angle of 35 degrees running to a height of

37 feet above the top of the revetment, and on its crest a high wall of brick standing back, in horizontal distance, 68 feet from the revetment at its base. The effect when this was complete all around the town must have been staggering.

The second is farther towards the edge of the mound and is not so clear, as it has lost most of its plaster, while the third and last scarp had at its foot a massive stone revetment still standing 15½ feet high, made of large and carefully fitted stones.

The tombs of this period are remarkable in that the grave goods are better preserved than at any other time. Usually they re-used the tombs of the previous people, the tomb-chamber being sealed by a large stone and the shaft filled in. The reason for the good preservation of objects would seem to be that gases seeped up through cracks in the rock, accumulated in the chamber and destroyed the germs of decay. So there are wooden tables, baskets, chairs, couches, wigs, even lumps of meat offerings, in a remarkable state of preservation. One of the Middle Bronze Age tombs is illustrated in Plate 26A. On the left can be seen a basket containing toilet accessories, and beside that is a three-legged table over five feet long on which was much food as well as a shallow wooden bowl that held a leg of mutton. To the right is the frame of a bed on which lies a skeleton, and around the walls were jars, plates and goblets; seven individuals were buried in this chamber. There has, of course, been a certain amount of disintegration, but these various articles of furniture can be reconstructed accurately on paper and give an idea of what the interior of houses must have looked like then. All the tombs contained multiple burials, and earlier skeletons and offerings were pushed into the corners of the tombs to make room for the latest arrivals. One of these tombs has been reconstructed exactly as found, in the Palestine Archaeological Museum in Jerusalem.

The people responsible for these new defenses and the tombs were most probably the Hyksos or Shepherd kings of the Bible. They are also credited with the introduction of the horse, and possibly the chariot, into Palestine and Egypt, and this would account for the new type of defense needed against a more mobile enemy than had been encountered before.

Iron Age

Of the subsequent history of Jericho there are now scarcely any remains on the mound; the most famous story associated with it—that of Joshua's attack on the town—is represented only by an odd pot or two and a few stumps of walls. Not even tombs of the period have yet been found. There certainly was a village of some kind on the mound then, but it has been entirely eroded away in all the areas so far examined. There was also some occupation of the site during the Iron Age, and houses have been found low down on the slopes of the mound well outside all the earlier defense walls. In Roman times the site of Jericho was moved to its present one, and only a few burials of the time are found on the mound. Probably the Romans and certainly the Byzantines dug into the mound for material for their mud bricks, and so helped the process of natural erosion which erased the remains of so many Jerichos.

Chapter X

THIS SITE is more than 1 mile north of Jericho, and is best reached by a road which turns off beside the police station in the town. When excavation was first started there in 1937 it was believed to be the remains of a church, possibly that of Gilgal, the whereabouts of which was much disputed, but the first few days' work showed that this was no church. As work proceeded it became clear that it must be a palace of some sort, and the pottery suggested an Umayyad date. This was later confirmed by finding two letters written on pieces of marble and addressed to Hisham, Commander of the Faithful, who could only be the Caliph Hisham ibn abd al Malik, who ruled the Arab Empire, which then stretched from India to Spain, from A.D. 724 to 743. It is still possible that there was originally a church on the site, for some of the pillars used in the inner court have crosses carved on them. Excavation of the main buildings continued up to 1948, and the establishment as now revealed includes a palace, a mosque, baths, colonnaded forecourt and an ornamental pool (Plate 27A). Excavation is now going on in another building to the north, from which it would appear that this was the domestic quarters for servants and slaves.

KHIRBAT AL MAFJAR

Originally the whole installation was enclosed in a walled estate or park, which probably included a game reserve where the ruler could hunt in comfort. Parts of the enclosure wall can be traced here and there, and suggest that it extended over a mile in the direction of the River Jordan: its limits on the north and south are less easy to determine. There being no spring in the immediate vicinity, water was brought from the springs at Nuaimah, some 2 miles to the northwest, which involved spanning two valleys with bridges. One of these still carries the water channel which irrigates the area between the spring and Mafjar, and in ancient times the flow of water was utilized at two points to turn flour mills. Remains of one of these can be seen about 100 yards west of the palace.

Mafjar is not the only Umayyad palace in the Jordan valley, for there is another at Khirbat Minyah near Tiberias, and there are many others in the deserts of Syria and Jordan. But it was the most elaborately planned and lavishly decorated of them all; the walls were covered not merely with frescoes but also with carved plaster (stucco) and statuary in the same medium. The builders and decorators must have been drawn from the Byzantine, Syrian and Mesopotamian areas, for elements of the art and architecture of all these countries are included. The building was never completed, but was none the less occupied for a considerable period, as the furring up of the hot-water pipes in the baths shows. It is unlikely, however, that the caliph himself ever stayed there. The whole place was destroyed by earthquake within a few years, probably the great one of A.D. 747, which destroyed also the Church of the Holy Sepulcher in Jerusalem and many of the buildings of Jarash. Thereafter the site was abandoned except for squatters during the twelfth century A.D., when a certain amount of hurried reconditioning was carried out in such parts as were inhabitable. Like many another ancient site, it provided a wonderful quarry for dressed stones when Jericho was being rebuilt in the early nineteenth century, and much damage was done then both to the structure and the sculpture. Some walls exist now only as foundation trenches, all the stone having been dug away.

While the building was under construction, many changes both in plan and decoration were constantly being made, and must have been a source of great worry to the contractors of the period. Neither the baths nor the mosques seem to have been part of the original plan, for they are but loosely connected with the palace, which must have been the main structure. And often much labor would be expended on carving some elaborate molding in stone, only to be covered in plaster and a painted decoration added on top of it. Walls would be plastered and carved in most elaborate patterns, and then busts and figures added on top of that. It is interesting, as I have remarked earlier, that in these early days of Islam there was no objection to the portrayal of animal and human figures, both in the round and in painting, and at Mafjar there is one statue which is probably a figure of the caliph himself.

The Ruins

The palace part of the installation is a square building—or rather was intended to be square, but has somehow got out of true. The basic plan was that of a typical Roman fortress; even the half-round towers at intervals along the outer wall were included, but with no thought for their military significance. There was an elaborate colonnaded forecourt which extended to the northern limits of the baths, and in the center of the court was the chief feature, an ornamental pool. The main entrance to the court was on the south, where it was entered by a gate flanked by two towers. These were originally planned as square towers, but the plan was changed, and they assumed their present curious shape. The gateway was paved with flagstones and had benches on either side. The court was enclosed on the south and east sides by an outer wall and a colonnade, but of this only the foundations remain, except for a small section on the west of the entrance gate where the pedestals for the columns still exist. Most of the area of the court seems to have been left bare, as, except for the drains running across the center from the palace and the pool, the soil is undisturbed.

The ornamental pool was a most curious structure, consisting of a square tank or pool about 3 feet deep covered by a massive octagonal pavilion, which was elaborately carved and decorated.

There was a fountain in the center of the tank, above which was a dome carried on four huge arches; these were decorated on the face with carved "wind-blown" acanthus leaves painted in red and yellow. The soffit, or flat area below the arch, was plastered and painted to represent marble and porphyry. The

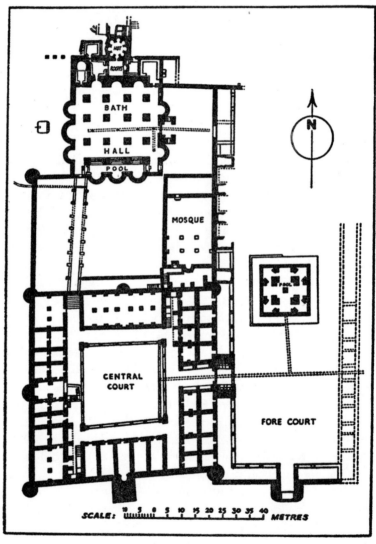

Fig. 10. Plan of Khirbat al Mafjar

piers for the arches, and for the octagonal structure which covered the remainder of the pool, rest in the water, the area of which is thus reduced to something small. Unfortunately the place has been badly plundered for stone, and the carved and decorated fragments remaining present many problems as to how this most unusual building was finished off. A balustrade of carved stones partly reconstructed on the west wall apparently ran around the roof of the octagon on the outside.

The main building of the palace was two stories high, and on the façade overlooking the courtyard were arcaded verandas on each story, on either side of the entrance. The ground-floor arcades were supported on clusters of four engaged columns standing on a rather high base; all these bases were found *in situ*. In the earthquake the arches had been flung down into the forecourt and were found lying more or less in position. Two of the clustered columns have been reconstructed, and the arches with the capitals are laid out on the ground near the present entrance. The first-floor arcades were supported on marble and granite columns, between which were elaborate balustrades of carved plaster: these arches are also laid out on the ground, in their relative position to those of the ground floor.

The entrance gate was in a large tower, the façade of which was decorated with carved stone in an interlacing pattern; these now lie in front of the entrance. There were also hexagonal medallions which presumably fitted into the scheme somewhere; two of these have been reconstructed on either side of the gate. The gate was surmounted by an elaborate arch, the front of which was decorated with a row of round-headed niches between radiating colonnettes; these latter were carried around under the archway and continued on to form a ribbed vault. All these stones are again laid out on the ground, so far as possible, in order. The tops of the walls of the whole place were crowned with zigzag crenelations, two of which have been reconstructed on top of the partly rebuilt wall of the gate tower. Within the entrance were benches on either side, behind which were niches with finely carved heads, fragments of which are now reconstructed on the benches.

The jambs of the main door are decorated in square panels,

and these are carried over the lintel, which consisted of three large stones. The passage immediately within the door was originally vaulted in brick, and a fragment of this vaulting can be seen in the room immediately to the south. There were more benches on either side of this passage, and the walls and clusters of columns were all plastered and elaborately carved. Immediately inside is the central courtyard, around which all the rooms were grouped, and which all opened onto. There was a cloister all around it, and many of the columns lie as they fell after the earthquake, some shattered to pieces. It is some of these columns that have crosses carved on them in relief, and they have clearly come from a church somewhere in the vicinity. The second story was reached by stairs in the northeast and southwest corners of the court. There was also an arcade on this story, the arches of which were supported on marble columns; between these were carved balustrades, some of which were never completed.

In the center of the southern side is a room which has a niche in its south wall, and this is probably the prayer niche in a small private mosque. Outside are the foundations of a large square tower which may have been a minaret. The whole of the north side of the court is occupied by one large room, the roof of which was supported on a series of arches. In the center of the west side, opposite the entrance, is another large room, which one would expect to be the hall of audience, because of its central position, but any sort of ceremonial approach to it is ruled out by the fact that the greater part of its entrance door overhangs a sunken court, and in order to get into it at all one would have to squeeze around the edge of the balustrade which protects this court. In the center of the main court a large, circular, stone window has been reconstructed. The fragments which compose it were found in this sunken court, and it would seem therefore to have been a window on the upper story above the room just referred to.

The sunken court is a curious affair: stairs lead down from the cloisters to an area paved with rather poor mosaic, and from here a door leads into what can only be an underground bathing establishment, for at the far end of the vaulted room is a plastered tank with a pipe coming out high up in the wall behind it. The walls and vault are all plastered, and the floor is of mosaic: there are benches on either side. There is also a deep drainage channel running out under the west wall, which could be reached by masonry shafts, three of which have been found outside the palace. The edges of the stairwell are protected by balustrades supported on onion-topped posts: they are identical to the screens which separate the nave from the chancel in Byzantine churches, and may have come from the same place as the carved columns. Perhaps this little room was intended to be the main bathing establishment before the great baths were added to the plan.

In the northwest corner of the court is a shallow flight of stairs leading to what was a covered passageway which gave private access to the baths. In a room at the beginning of these stairs can be seen some roofing tiles stacked against the end wall, either left over from the main building or never used; they are of red pottery. It seems from this that the palace must have had a pent roof of red tiles, which would have given it a strange appearance.

On the east, between the palace and the baths, is the mosque. The only approach to it that can be seen from the plan is by way of a passage leading off from that which goes to the baths; at the end of the passage is a flight of stairs leading up, another leading down on the other side, and finally a small door with steps which lead into the mosque just beside the *mihrab* or prayer niche. The whole layout is so extraordinary that one gets the impression that the builders were merely improvising as they went along, without any coherent plan to work to. The mosque is typical of the earliest known examples of such structures, being a rectangular enclosure open to the sky except for an arched and roofed space at the south end, which sheltered the *mihrab* and a small area in front of it. There is no sign of a minaret.

The baths are the most elaborate part of the whole establishment, consisting of a forecourt, an entrance porch, a huge hall 100 feet square with a pool on the south side, hot rooms, cool rooms and a steam room, and in the northwest corner a very special retiring room. The hall has three apses in each of the north, west and south walls, and two in the east wall, where is also the entrance. These apses were roofed, at a considerable height, with semi-domes. The roof was supported on sixteen vast piers of clustered engaged columns and pilasters. These piers carried large arches, over each of which was a row of three windows, while in the wall-faces between the windows were small niches, plastered and painted to represent marble and porphyry. The roof was at least partly vaulted with brick, except for the central section, where a dome soared up some height above the rest of it. The whole floor area was paved with mosaics, every apse and almost every square having a different geometric pattern. It represents the largest single area of ancient mosaic so far known. Except for damage from falling masonry it is intact (Plate 28A).

The entrance porch was a small square room with wall arches on every side; in the corners were pendentives which supported a dome. The whole was completely covered in carved stucco. The pendentives consist of male figures supporting a band of acanthus leaves on top of which is a frieze of seated sheep in the round. Above this is the drum of the dome in which were ten or perhaps twelve niches. In each niche stood alternate male and female figures, the men wearing loincloths and the women skirts from the waist down. The women also have necklaces, earrings and a rosette in the hair, while some carry bouquets or baskets of flowers. All were painted in bright colors. The façade of the porch was also covered in carved stucco and had two niches, one on either side of the entrance; from one of these came a male figure wearing a long red robe, carrying a sword, and standing on a pair of squatting lions. This is the figure which is believed to be that of the Caliph Hisham; it is displayed in the Jerusalem museum.

In the walls of the hall and of the apses were rows of niches at two levels; the central apse on the west was more elaborately treated than the others. Here the lower row of niches are horseshoe-shaped, flanked by colonnettes and have carved heads, whereas those of the other apses have only plain, square niches. Also the niches of the upper row had colonnettes decorated with carved plaster, and each contained a statue. From the center of the semi-dome of this apse a stone pendant hung on a stone chain, the whole carved out of a single block of stone. Further, the mosaic floor here is more elaborate than in the other apses, being a variation on the pattern found in the central square.

On the south side a flight of steps between the piers leads to the swimming pool or cold plunge: this was clearly an afterthought, for neither the steps nor the walls of the pool bond into the piers or to the main walls.

The little room in the northwest corner was obviously of special importance, for it has the finest mosaic floor in the building and was the most elaborately decorated of them all. It consists of two parts: the front, which is square, with benches down two sides, and the back part, which is a semi-circular alcove or apse and the floor of which is at a higher level than that of the front. The mosaic in the front part is made in imitation of a carpet, having a geometric design and a tassel represented at each corner. The floor of the apse, however, shows a tree with fruits, all very delicately shaded, on the left of which two gazelles are grazing, while on the right a lion attacks another gazelle (Plate 27B). The design, colors and shading are clearly copied from a tapestry original, and a band of tassels all around it confirms this. It is most beautifully and delicately executed, and as the stones of which it is made are only half the size of those used in the main hall, very fine degrees of shading can be produced. Both floors here, apart from one tiny patch, are undamaged, in contrast to that of the hall, where the falling masonry has crashed right into the floor in some parts and most of it is more or less damaged, though none is missing.

The walls of this room were covered in carved stucco, some of which remains round the base of the apse walls: the apse itself was apparently roofed with a semi-dome, also plastered. The square part of the room had a complete dome, with pendentives in the form of medallions of flying horses. Above this was a frieze of carved and painted partridges, and in the drum were pierced and carved plaster windows; some at least of these had colored glass in them. The flat dome had a wide band of intertwining vine pattern around the edge, and in the center a rosette from which six leaves radiate. Between each of the leaves is a human head, alternately male and female, the males being bearded and the females wearing earrings; they were also painted, the hair black, and the men a dark brown and the women much lighter. Immediately behind them is an elaborate openwork scroll of vine tendrils and leaves (Plate 28B).

The cool and hot rooms to the north have suffered badly from the depredations of stonehunters, particularly as they were floored and lined with marble. The first two rooms one enters from the hall are the tepidaria or cool rooms, from the first of which a door leads into the two hot rooms. The floors of these have gone, and so, recently, has the elaborate brick heating system below them. The first hot room is square and has its furnace on the east side, from which the heat passed by brick flues under the floor and up the walls through pottery pipes some of which can still be seen. On the east side was a niche over the furnace which contained a water tank to heat the water for the steam room. The north room is circular and has eight horse-shoe-shaped niches. The five nearest the door were, like the rest of the room, heated by hot air from beneath the floor, whereas the other three were over the furnace, which was on the north, and had hot-water tanks in them. Firing of both furnaces was done from outside, each being approached by flights of steps.

The steam room was to the east, and a water channel runs around three sides of it, above which is a bench pierced with rectangular slots at regular intervals to allow the steam to rise into the room. There was a small fountain, probably of cold water, in the center of the room, and the floor is covered with plain white mosaic.

Much of the carved plaster from these buildings has been reconstructed in the Palestine Archaeological Museum in Jerusalem and is on show there. Being very friable, it cannot be left on the site in the open, particularly as much of it is painted.

Chapter XI

THIS LITTLE RUIN, on the shores of the Dead Sea about
8 miles south of Jericho, is now world famous as the site from
which the Dead Sea Scrolls originated. When knowledge of the
existence of these unique manuscripts first became fairly general
in 1948–1949, Qumran was known only to a few archaeologists,
and not many of them had actually been to the site. It was first
visited and described by scholars towards the end of the last
century, and one of them, on account of a faint similarity of
name, even suggested it might be the site of Gomorrah. The
study of potsherds and stratigraphy had not then become as
accurate as it now is, and no modern archaeologist seeing the site
before excavation would have dated it earlier than Roman.

The Dead Sea Scrolls

The story of the original discovery of the first examples of
the Dead Sea Scrolls has been described many times and with
many variations. I still believe the original account as told to me
in the early summer of 1949 by the two shepherds concerned,
and published in the London *Times* of August 9 of that year, to
be the true one, for they had not then any need or incentive
either to conceal or elaborate the account. Briefly, it is that while

pasturing their flocks of goats by the foothills on the northwest shores of the Dead Sea in the summer of 1947, the younger of the two shepherds missed one of his goats, and while searching for it up one of the steep side valleys he saw a circular hole in the rock. Idle curiosity prompted him to look more closely at this hole which was in a vertical face of rock at about eye level; he could see nothing except that there was apparently a cave or empty space within, so he picked up a stone and threw it through the hole. Great was his surprise—and fear—when he heard it strike, and apparently shatter, something within, and he hurriedly left the spot, only to return a day or so later with his older companion (Plate 29A). Braving the terrors of the unknown, they climbed in through the hole, and found themselves in a narrow cleft in the rock, on either side of which were some tall jars— they seem to remember four on one side and five on the other— with bowls inverted over their necks as covers. One had been broken by the stone the boy had thrown in. Examination of the jars showed them all to be empty except one, which had three rolls of old leather in it on which apparently was writing. Rather disgusted that they were not filled with gold, the shepherds stuffed the leather rolls into the bosom of their garments and left the cave. These curious rolls were shown to friends and relations, one of whom gave me a vivid description of how when the largest was unrolled it stretched from one end of their tent to the other—from which we can identify it as the now famous Scroll of Isaiah, some 23 feet long.

The subsequent adventures of these three Scrolls is still far from clear, but eventually they found their way to people who were able to assess, more or less, their true importance. Palestine was unfortunately in the throes of fighting and the winding up of the mandate at this time, and clandestine excavation of the cave— now known as Cave I—was carried out by the people who had acquired the first scrolls. Some of them were shown to the American School of Oriental Research in Jerusalem, where they were photographed, and the first thing I knew of them was a brief notice which appeared in the *Bulletin* of that school which reached me in November 1948. It was clear even from this short account that here was a find of the very first importance, and that the cave must be excavated as soon as possible. The problem was to find it, and it was not until things were a little quieter in January 1949 that a small detachment of the Arab Legion was able to investigate the probable area of the cave and to rediscover it. When I was told the news a small expedition was hurriedly organized, consisting of Père de Vaux, director of the École Biblique et Archaeologique Française of Jerusalem, one worker from Amman and two from the Palestine Archaeological Museum, and myself, and proceeded to the site. After thorough and exhaustive examination and excavation of Cave I we were still faced with two major problems: what was the real date of the Scrolls, and from where did they originate? We had recovered many small fragments of scrolls and a great quantity of pottery, and considered that on the evidence of ninety-five percent of the latter they must be pre-Roman in date, probably first century B.C., for the greater part of the vessels were large cylindrical jars with bowl-like covers, forms which had not been encountered in any Roman sites in the country. However, there were a few other sherds which built up into a typical Roman cooking pot and parts of two Roman lamps; these were tentatively assigned to the second century A.D., and proved at first a great stumbling block.

Among the various objects recovered from Cave I was a quantity of linen, and some of this was submitted to the carbon 14 test for date; the result gave A.D. 33 plus or minus 200 years, thus giving a wide scope. There for some time the matter rested, and palaeographers and scholars argued the date on the form of the letters and contents of such scrolls as were available for study.

We all believed at the time that this cave was unique, that there never could or would be another discovery like it, so it was clearly of great importance to try to find some more definite means of dating the Scrolls and also to try to find their place of origin. A fresh examination of the surface sherds at Qumran— the only ancient site anywhere in the neighborhood—seemed to confirm that it was of Roman date, and what could be seen of the building itself looked very much like the ruins of a small fort.

173

However, there was no alternative site, and so in 1951 it was decided to make a trial excavation there. Three rooms in the southwest corner of the main building were chosen for the experiment, and as it turned out the choice was a lucky one, for when floor level of one of the rooms was reached, there, buried in the floor with which its mouth was level, was a jar identical with those found in the cave, and beside it was a coin of A.D. 10. At the same time many Roman-type lamps and other vessels were found. It was clear that there must be a direct connection with the cave, and, moreover, that there was a good chance of reaching a reasonably accurate date.

By the end of 1949 stories of the fabulous value of the Scrolls had begun to appear in the Press, and the Bedu who made the original discovery—not having made much out of it themselves—decided to try their luck at finding further caves and scrolls. The territory over which the Bedu roam is a very wild and barren one, being the area between Bethlehem and the Dead Sea, and it would be very difficult for anyone not well acquainted with the district to find his way about without one of them to guide him. It is rocky, desolate country, and a few people wishing to hide themselves there could avoid detection even though a whole army were searching for them. Most of the Bedu had been shepherds when they were young, and remembered many caves and holes in the rock in which they had sheltered in those early days, so they returned and proceeded to search them for possible manuscripts. They were soon successful, and early in 1951 located in some large caves at Murabbaat, about 11 miles south of Qumran, a deposit of inscribed leather and papyrus. These turned out to be some seventy years later than the Qumran Scrolls, but were nevertheless of very great interest.

Almost at the same time another contingent working the Qumran area found another cave with a few inscribed fragments of leather in it, clearly of the same date and type as the scrolls from Cave I. We were excavating the Murabbaat caves then, so as soon as our work there was done we had to hurry back to Qumran and examined a whole series of thirty-seven caves in the cliff face there. In only one did we find any inscribed material, and this consisted of two rolls of copper with clear traces on the outside of Hebrew characters which had been hammered onto the inner face. But in almost every cave entered we found potsherds of the same type as those from Cave I, which showed they had at least been occupied. In December of that year the first trial excavation at Qumran was carried out, and continued on a much larger scale for about three months each year until 1956, by which time the whole of the installation had been laid bare and an accurate dating, based on the evidence of more than 400 coins, had been established.

But it was in the autumn of 1952 that the Bedu made their greatest discovery, that of Cave IV (the second cave at Qumran had been called Cave II and that with the copper rolls Cave III): this cave produced the largest quantity of manuscript material yet seen, though it was all fragmentary. The reason for this was that instead of storing the Scrolls in jars as had been done in Cave I, they were merely laid on the floor of the cave, and so had been subjected to the action of damp, soil salts, and the depredations of white ants and rats. Cave IV is a mere 100 yards from the ruin of Qumran, and it was humiliating to us—and to the workers—to think that we had been there every day for three weeks earlier that spring and had not suspected the existence of the cave (Plates 31A and 31B).

The History of Qumran

We can now say, on the basis of the archaeological and coin evidence, that the history of the site—and consequently of the Scrolls—is as follows. It started life as a fortress in the Iron Age, probably about the seventh century B.C., and many sherds of this period and even one ostracon were found. It was then apparently abandoned until the second century B.C., when a group of people decided to retire to some place remote from the world, there to pursue their own religious life and teachings, which were somewhat out of conformity with the orthodox Jewish life of Jerusalem. They chose Qumran, and built their new center partly on the foundations of the Iron Age fort, but extended considerably beyond that on the south and the west. The site was well n, standing as it does on a spur of land some 250 feet above level of the Dead Sea, and protected on the south by the steep rp of the Wadi Qumran, on the west by the cliff above which the Judaean desert and on the east by the slopes which run down to the foreshore of the Dead Sea. Only on the north was it open, but even from there it was not easy to approach, and although they were unwarlike people they nevertheless took defensive precautions. They installed an elaborate system of water cisterns and sumps, building a channel to bring the rainwater from the waterfalls in the Wadi Qumran, for they had to rely entirely on rain for their supplies. They made themselves a completely self-contained community, even having their own potters' quarters and kilns, and probably grew such fruit and vegetables as they needed on the marshy lands by the Dead Sea between Qumran and Feshkha to the south. The sect would appear to have attracted more and more disciples, for there is evidence even in the first building of alterations and enlargements.

They would seem to have pursued a quiet and peaceful existence there for about a century, when some episode occurred which caused them to abandon the place for a time. Evidence was found in the excavations of a great earthquake, which was so severe that the main building was split in two, and the eastern half sank nearly 18 inches below the western. Such violence must have thrown down the rest of the building at the same time, and again there is ample evidence for this. The date of this earthquake can be fixed with considerable certainty from two different sources: the coins found in the excavations and the historian Josephus. The coins follow an unbroken sequence from the earliest of John Hyrcanus (135–104 B.C.) up to Herod the Great (about 36 B.C.): of the latter ruler, under whom Palestine attained a considerable degree of prosperity, only five coins have been found, a circumstance which would be hard to explain if the place was occupied during his reign. Josephus tells us that when Herod was in Jericho with his army in the spring of 31 B.C. there was a great and violent earthquake which caused a panic among his troops. The date fits the coin evidence very nicely, but whether it was the earthquake or some other event that caused the abandonment of the settlement cannot definitely be decided now. On the face of it, an earthquake would hardly seem enough reason for leaving a flourishing place, though it might have been regarded as indicating the wrath of God for some misdemeanor.

Whatever the cause, the settlement was unoccupied from at least 31 B.C. until about 4 B.C., which is the date of the first of the next sequence of coins. A rather curious confirmation of the abandonment and of the date of rebuilding was discovered in one of the rooms on the west, where, just below the floor level, were found three small pots containing a hoard of some 570 silver coins; one of the pots was immediately inside the doorway. These coins range in date from 135 B.C., to 5 B.C., and represented a considerable fortune in those days. They could hardly have been hidden while the place was occupied, for no one wishing to conceal anything would bury it just inside the door; rather they would choose the corner of a room. And the dates fit remarkably well.

Anyhow, about 4 B.C. the sect returned, cleared out the ruin of the buildings and proceeded to put the establishment in order again. The debris which they removed was dumped in a side wadi to the north, and even if the earthquake had caused the abandonment, it would explain why no bodies were found in the ruins. They restored the original building, and domestic installations included a flour mill and bakery, bins for storing grain, potters' kilns and a pit for levigating the clay, and a furnace perhaps for metallurgy. It would appear that some members of the sect must have inhabited the various natural caves in the cliff face, and other caves were cut in the soft marl in the immediate vicinity of the settlement; many of the latter had stairways leading down to them.

In A.D. 66 the first Jewish revolt against the Romans started, and grew to such proportions that some legions had to be moved into the country to suppress it. Whether the people of the settlement took any active or political part in the revolt is not known, but it would seem unlikely. However, there they were, a small, isolated and almost undefended community, and the legions did not bother to distinguish between one group of Jews and another, so in A.D. 68 or 69 the settlement was sacked and burnt, and the inhabitants probably massacred. But they must have had warning of the approach of the Romans (we know from Josephus that it was the tenth legion at Jericho), and hurriedly hid their most valued possession—their library—in some of the nearby caves. Remains of more than four hundred different scrolls have so far been identified—quite a considerable library for those days —and it is by no means sure that this represented the entire contents. No doubt someone hoped to return and rescue the manuscripts, but this was never done. On the ruins of part of the main building of the settlement, 6 feet above the floor level of some rooms, the Romans established a small post, and from coins found in their rooms the place seems to have been mantained up to the end of the first century. Thereafter it was left alone, but at least the tower at the northwest corner remained fairly clear, for in a hole in the floor of the basement part of it, which here is the native marl, was found a group of coins of the second Jewish revolt of A.D. 132–135. Apparently it was one of the rebel hideouts, of which there were many in the barren wilderness of Judea.

This was no more than a temporary occupation, and except for a few squatters or perhaps passing shepherds in early Arab times, the site was totally abandoned, and remained so until recently excavated. But the area was not entirely neglected, and we are given one more glimpse of it in about A.D. 800, when a certain Timotheus, Patriarch of Baghdad-Seleucia, wrote a letter to Sergius, Metropolitan of Elam, saying that a certain person from Jerusalem had recently visited him and told him a strange story. It appeared that an Arab had been out hunting with his dog in the vicinity of Jericho, and the dog, in pursuit of some wild animal, disappeared into a hole in the rock; as he did not return for some time his master went in after him. He found himself in what the patriarch described as a little house in the rock, in which were many manuscripts. He reported his find to some Jewish scholars in Jerusalem, who came down to the cave and removed many of the scrolls, which were reported as being books of the

Old Testament and other Hebrew works. The story can only refer to one of the Qumran caves.

It is fairly generally accepted now that the sect who lived at Qumran was that of the Essenes, about whom Josephus tells us a good deal. They are also mentioned by another writer of the time, Pliny the Elder. The latter's description of the position of their settlement on the shores of the Dead Sea resembles so closely that of Qumran, that this alone would be sufficient to suggest an identification. The contents of the Scrolls seem to confirm that they are writings of the Essenes, though there are still some scholars who are unwilling to accept the identification. So far, however, no other proposal has been made which so well fits all the known archaeological facts, especially those of dating.

The Ruins

It will be seen from the air photograph (Plate 30) that there are three main entrances to the present remains: one just north of the tower (32), one in the long east wall, and one at the southwest corner. There was also a door in the south wall of the long room on the south, but this was blocked up in the final phase. The Romans had a door (1) by the northeast corner of the tower and another beside the cracked cistern (2).

Entering by the door to the northwest of the tower (3), one finds oneself in an open courtyard (4), from which a door on the right led to a much larger court. Running diagonally across these courtyards is the main drain, covered with slabs of stone, and emptying into the little wadi to the north. Beyond these courts to the west is a stepped cistern (5), and beside it what appears to be a system of sluice gates for controlling the flow of water from the channel. In front of the cistern is a large open space (6) in which, apparently, the mud was first allowed to settle before the water was run off into the main channel which supplied all the other cisterns. Returning to the tower, remains of another gateway lead through south into a rectangular open courtyard (7), partly cobbled and partly plastered. The main building now lies to the east and the additional domestic quarters to the west.

There are two doors in the wall of the main building here, giving access to different parts of it; that to the north (8) leads into the central part, and that on the south (9) to a group of rooms which seem to have had some special significance. It is not easy now to say what purpose the various rooms of the central part served, for many of them were re-used by the Roman legions, but perhaps room (10) was the kitchen. Tucked away in a corner of (11) is what was clearly a bathroom of some kind; the walls and floors are plastered, and a drain runs out under the east wall. The function of some of the plaster structure here is very obscure. The southern door gives access to a passageway, on the south of which is a flight of steps leading up to the first floor; this part of the building at least had two stories, as had also some parts of the domestic quarters.

To the east is a long, narrow room (12), in which was made one of the most interesting finds. Mixed up in the debris along the east side of this room was a large quantity of plastered mud brick, which had clearly fallen from the upper story. It was a strange shape, having a flat upper surface and curved sides which narrowed considerably towards the base; behind it were remains of a sort of low plastered bench. The fragments, large and small, were carefully collected, and when pieced together in the Jerusalem museum turned out to be a long, tablelike structure with the low bench behind it. Mixed up in this plaster and brick had been found two inkwells, one bronze and one of pottery, the bronze one still containing a quantity of dried ink. It would seem likely, therefore, that this was the remains of the scriptorium, where scribes sat and copied the Scrolls, though it must have been an exceedingly uncomfortable job at such a desk.

The room on the south of the passage must have been some sort of place of assembly (13), for a low plaster bench, like that of the scriptorium, runs round all four sides of the room, and the floor is also plastered. Immediately inside the doorway on the left is a plastered niche and basin in the wall, with a small plastered channel going through the wall into the passage, by which a supply of water could be maintained in the basin without any outside person interrupting whatever was going on inside. Three square niches in the south wall were probably cupboards, though they seem at one time to have gone right through the wall and opened into the adjoining room. Originally the room had a door at the west end of the south wall, but this was blocked up in the latest stage. The two rooms to the south are of uncertain use, and that on the west was an afterthought, as its wall does not bond in with the main walls.

At the south end of the court separating the two buildings can be seen the remains of the large bread oven (14), and beyond it on the other side of the water channel the cobbled floor where the flour mill stood in the last phase (15). The mill itself, made of black volcanic stone, is outside the building to the south. Nearby is one of the largest cisterns in the place (16), with a flight of steps leading down into it and a sump for clearing the water beside it. Immediately to the east is another large cistern, also with steps, but divided in two by a wall across its width (17, 18); it is difficult to see any reason for this division. The water channel continues along the north side of this cistern, and has to be followed in order to gain access to the eastern part of the building. Here is yet another stepped cistern (19), which shows more clearly and dramatically than anything else the effect of the earthquake of 31 B.C., for it is cracked diagonally across its length and the eastern side had dropped nearly 18 inches below the western side (Plate 31c). The continuation of this crack can be seen in a small cistern adjoining to the north, and runs right through the remaining cross walls of the building. To the east of the stepped cistern is another bathroom or washing place (20). Beneath the steps of the cistern can be seen the remains of a large potters' kiln, but beyond the fact that it must belong to an early phase of the building it is not possible to assign it to a definite period.

The water channel curves around the east end of the cistern and continues east to feed two small cisterns, the first of which is again damaged by earthquake, and finally empties into the very large stepped cistern at the southeast corner (21). Outside the building area here is a pit and a large, shallow, plastered basin in which clay for making pottery was levigated or cleaned (22), the water being tapped from the main channel. Two pottery kilns, one large and one small, stand near the eastern outer wall (23). From the large cistern a wall runs south along the edge of the spur of land as far as the scarp of the Wadi Qumran, and provided an additional defense for the place. The open area here (24) is all artificial accumulation, nearly 4 feet deep in some parts, and many large jars containing the remains of ritual feasts were found buried here.

Room (25) is the largest in the settlement, and was probably the place of worship or congregation. Towards the west end, just in front of a door leading to a side room, a small circular area is paved with slabs of stone, and it may be that the reader or head of the community stood here during ceremonies. The adjoining room to the south was in the latest phase divided into three, and in the most southerly one (26) was found a great store of pottery, more than a thousand vessels, beakers, plates, bowls and jars.

The domestic quarters on the west include three more cisterns (27–29), one of them a circular one, which is perhaps the earliest on the site, for the original water channel, some 2 feet below the level of the present one, empties directly into it and can be seen in the north side. The other two cisterns are the usual rectangular stepped ones. In a room adjoining the circular cistern on the north (30) are the remains of two clay bins, probably used for storing grain. The remaining rooms on the west have been altered many times, but seem originally to have been three long, narrow chambers. The north one (31) is now divided into three, that on the west being peculiar in that there is no means of access to it. The wall, crudely built in a mixture of stone and mud brick, has only two narrow slits in it. It was immediately inside the original door of this long room that the hoard of silver coins already referred to was found.

There is now no visible means of access to the rooms in the tower (32), but it may have been approached from the roof or the first floor. It was also two stories high, and consisted of a basement, with neither doors nor windows giving onto the outside, and an upper floor of which only a few traces now remain. The curious little room in the southwest corner with the free-standing pillar in the center may have had a wooden spiral staircase giving access to the basement. The tower suffered badly in the earthquake, and a shattered door lintel can be seen in room (33); and a sloping revetment had to be added all around its base in order to make it stable.

The quality of the building generally is very poor, and whatever class of people the sect attracted they do not seem to have included architects and masons. At some time during its occupation there was a colonnade in the building, for bases and column drums have been found scattered throughout the ruins, but this may only have been a plan which was never carried out, for some of the stones do not appear to have been finished off. The continuous changing of plan, dividing up of rooms, enlarging here, reducing there, adding fresh coats of plaster to cover up the botching, and so on, makes the problem of sorting out the different phases an extremely difficult one; nor does the pottery help much, for throughout its life there was little change in the local forms and types.

The famous Cave IV is very close to the settlement, in the spur immediately to the west of that on which are the buildings, and on the extreme edge of the wadi scarp (Plate 31A). Those who do not mind a bit of a scramble and have a head for heights can easily visit it. Some rough steps have now been cut in the marl, which make approach easier, and they lead to a small hole which was the original entrance to the series of caves. A low passage runs for a short distance, then drops down suddenly to a lower level, from which again there is a fall into the cave itself. The larger openings by these two drops were made by the Bedu when they were excavating there, but they did not find the original entrance. Cave IV has been entirely excavated artificially, and the sides slope inwards for greater stability. Adjoining it on the south, at a slightly higher level, are the remains of another cave, most of which has eroded away, while on the west there is a drop into yet another, half of which has been eroded away into the gully which at this point cuts back into the marl. Looking across this gully, two more caves can be seen, which may originally have been independent, as they have their own way of access from the next spur to the west. A large hole in the floor of Cave IV suggests that it may have been intended to make yet another cave there, but this was never done. This hole had in the course of time been completely filled with debris, and so was missed by the Bedu who first cleared the cave, as they could not distinguish between the natural marl and the artificial fill, as could the trained workers. Many fragments of scrolls had found their way into this hole before it became filled up. The other caves are all in the rock face to the west, some distance from the settlement, and impossible to find without a guide.

In the last year of excavation the beginning of yet another large building was unearthed near the spring at Feshkha, to the south of Qumran, but so far only one room and part of another have been cleared, sufficient to establish the fact that it is contemporary with Qumran.

The main cemetery at Qumran lies on the flat land and the spurs to the east of the settlement. In this group there are more than a thousand graves, and other small groups of graves have been found to the north and south of the settlement. Most of the graves are oriented north and south, but there are some which are at right angles to this, east and west. Excavation of examples of both has shown no difference in the type of grave or burial, so the reason for this drastic change in orientation is a mystery. The graves consist of a shaft about 2 yards long by ½ yard wide by 2 yards deep; in one side of this shaft at the bottom is cut a shallow loculus in which the body was laid. The entrance to the loculus was then covered with either stones or bricks and the shaft filled, and a pile of stones erected over the grave with a standing stone at head and foot. Nothing was ever buried with the body, except at some graves of women and children south of the Wadi Qumran, where a few beads were found with the women. In two graves remains of wooden coffins were found.

In general the ruins of Qumran are not very exciting or impressive to look at, but their association with the Scrolls makes them of great interest and importance, and the settlement is, furthermore, almost the only building in the country which has survived unchanged, except for the natural processes of decay, since the time of Christ.

Chapter XII

THE DEPARTMENT OF ANTIQUITIES: ITS DUTIES AND RE-
SPONSIBILITIES · PROTECTION OF SITES · UNAUTHORIZED
SALE AND SMUGGLING OF ANTIQUITIES · REWARDS · AT-
TRACTION OF TOURISTS · PURCHASE OF DEAD SEA SCROLLS
FROM BEDU · CO-OPERATION OF FOREIGN INSTITUTIONS ·
REPAIRING, RESTORATION AND KEEPING OF RECORDS BY DE-
PARTMENT · NEED FOR TECHNICAL EXPERTS · JORDAN
ARCHAEOLOGICAL MUSEUM IN AMMAN · PALESTINE AR-
CHAEOLOGICAL MUSEUM IN JERUSALEM

THE FUNCTIONS of the Department of Antiquities have already been briefly referred to (p. 9), but it is not generally realized what a great variety of problems are involved in the administration and organization of such an undertaking, so that perhaps an expansion of the theme is not out of place.

In a country such as Jordan, which trusts and is generous to archaeological societies excavating under a government license, and grants them a fair share of their discoveries, there will never be a shortage of active excavation projects. But no society exists at present which would undertake in a foreign country the preservation, conservation and restoration of its ancient monuments. Most government Departments of Antiquities have to work with a pathetically small budget, so that every undertaking must be carefully considered; bearing this in mind, it is obviously the duty of the government to preserve already existing monuments so far as is possible and not, as a major policy, to indulge in excavation which may well bring still further problems. For it is by no means the end of the story when an excavation has

185

been completed; during the period of work a considerable quantity of objects will have been found, mainly pottery and mostly broken, and some important monumental structures may also have been revealed.

The department takes its share of the objects, and such as are broken or damaged must be cleaned, repaired and restored, whether they be of pottery, metal or any other material; they must also be catalogued, registered, photographed and—when suitable—prepared for exhibition in the museum. And if an important monument has been discovered it is the department's responsibility to preserve it *in situ*. Obviously, however, there are occasions when the department is fully justified in carrying out excavations, and one of these is when antiquities are found casually, say in the course of digging foundations for a building. In such a case the department must act promptly as soon as it receives news of the find, for if the contractor or owner of the site is kept hanging about for some time and prevented from continuing with the work, he will not disclose any future discoveries, and they will be broken up and lost. Usually the excavation involved in such a case is comparatively small, often unrewarding, but it must be attended to nonetheless.

Attracting visitors to a country where there are ancient sites is also part of the work of the department, so excavation at a site in order to improve its tourist amenities is also justified. When a site—such as Qumran, for example—is of immense importance and interest, then the department should take at least a share in the work of excavation, even if it cannot undertake the whole job itself. As a principle, however, conservation and preservation should be the major policy of the department. Jordan is blessed with more than its fair share of monuments of the past.

Antiquities guards have to be maintained on all the principal sites and in each administrative district of the country; they spend the greater part of their time touring around their district, mainly on horseback, seeing that the ancient sites both large and small are not being used as quarries for building-stone or made the object of unauthorized excavation. Often the areas covered by the guards are so large that a site cannot be visited more than once a year. That is, perhaps, better than nothing, but leaves an unfortunately long period of time for plunderers to do their work.

Most people are interested in antiquities for what they are worth in cash, having generally grossly exaggerated ideas of the value of any ancient piece; usually also they are shy of getting themselves in any way involved with the government, an attitude for which in the past they have had ample justification. The Antiquities Law quite rightly claims all antiquities and monuments as the property of the government, which has the authority to confiscate any object in connection with which some contravention of the law has taken place. Most travellers are unaware—as are many government officials also—of a further clause which states that anyone who accidentally finds an antiquity and promptly reports it to the authorities is entitled to adequate compensation if the government is desirous of acquiring it. But even when this latter provision is rigidly adhered to by the department, fear of the government often leads finders of objects to take them to a dealer rather than to the Department of Antiquities. Failure to pay an adequate price for casual finds will certainly ensure that nothing whatever is reported and that antiquities will be smuggled out of the country to some more lucrative market. In the not so distant past the smuggling of valuable ancient objects was a regular feature in every country in the world which yields such finds, as much in Europe as elsewhere, and while more enlightened administration has now reduced this risk considerably, it has by no means vanished entirely. There is particular risk when some find of outstanding importance is made, especially if the objects are of such a nature as to be easily transportable.

The Dead Sea Scrolls offer a very good example of this sort of problem; the initial find was made in Palestine at a time when that country was unfortunately in a disturbed state, and between the termination of the Mandate in May 1948 and a return to more peaceful conditions in 1949 several of the Scrolls from Cave I were smuggled to America. During the following two years the department in Jordan gradually made contact with the original finders of the cave, and by the time the second great find of Cave IV was made in 1952 the Bedu had sufficient trust in the good faith of the department to inform them, even though indirectly, of the discovery. An initial examination of some of the material showed that it was of great importance, and the stories told by the finders indicated that there was a very large quantity of manuscript fragments. It was not possible to see the find as a whole because the various parties of Bedu who cleared most of the cave each kept their share, and not all were completely trusting. However, on the basis of what could be seen, and making a rough estimate of the rest from the discoverers' accounts, it was estimated that £15,000 should be sufficient to acquire all the fragments. The department accordingly reported to the government and asked if this sum might be made available in order to acquire the fragments and so keep them all together in the country. The government, though its resources were indeed slender, rose to the occasion and provided the sum asked for.

Negotiations were started with the finders and their agents and a large quantity of fragments acquired. But when actual cash started being paid out, more and more fragments began to appear, and it soon became clear that there was at least twice the quantity originally estimated. The department, cap in hand, reported the situation to the government, who, however, were unable to find another £15,000 in the same year. So another scheme was proposed to them, namely, that foreign universities, museums and learned institutions should be invited to contribute to the cost of the rest of the material; these scrolls would have to remain in the country until they had been fully studied and prepared for publication, after which the contributing member would receive a share of the manuscript fragments proportionate to the amount subscribed. The government agreed to this plan, and a number of institutions sent their contributions. So, thanks to the generous and wise policy of the government, it acquired for the country the greatest share of the fragments and enabled the whole mass to be kept together in Jordan for study as a unit.

Fortunately it is not every day that a problem of this magnitude has to be faced.

The internal organization of the department itself is a highly complex affair. There must be technicians capable of cleaning, repairing and restoring the vast quantity of pottery which any excavation produces, others who can clean and repair ancient metal objects, bronze, copper, silver and so on, and ensure that after cleaning they will not be subject to further corrosive action. The photographic department always has about twice as much work on hand as it can competently deal with, and the photography of antiquities requires a very special technique. Registers of all the ancient sites in the country have to be maintained, with photographs, plans, and a bibliography wherever possible; these records must be kept up to date, and ideally should have a list of at least the registration number of all objects found in the site which are the property of the department, and a reference to the whereabouts of any others known to have originated from it. Every object acquired by the department has to be given a number and be entered in another register, with a description, photograph, details of date, place, present whereabouts and— when it has been published—a bibliography; keeping this register up to date, when several thousand objects may be acquired in a year, is no light task.

Archaeology, like other sciences, is becoming so highly specialized that it is impossible to have in one department a technician or expert capable of dealing with every contingency that may arise. The assistance of outside experts has therefore frequently to be called upon, and is always most generously given. But it is important that the department should have at least a core of trained workers, and it is this which the Jordan department has, up to the present, seriously lacked. No amount of amateur enthusiasm can substitute for proper technical training, though it can be and has been of the greatest assistance. A draftsman capable of drawing the pots, scarabs, tools, weapons, flints, bones and other multitudinous objects is an essential. It is rare that even a good artist can start in and draw a pot to scale accurately; the technique is quite different and requires a different approach. And in order to reproduce any inscription whatever, sufficiently accurate for an expert to be able to read it, at least a rough knowledge of the alphabet or script involved is essential to avoid the inclusion of odd scratches and marks which may appear to the untrained to be part of the text.

All this complex organization—and the above list by no means completes the tally—has to be administered and kept in working order by the director of the department, so it is necessary that he be first and foremost a good administrator. He should, of course, have some knowledge, if not of archaeology, then of history—for the aim of archaeology is to provide the daily background to history—in order properly to appreciate its needs. The Jordan department is at the moment fortunate in having such a man at its head, an excellent administrator and a historian. It is impossible to foresee what will be the trend of archaeological policy in the future, but it is earnestly to be hoped that the department will continue to trust and encourage foreign excavators and to maintain its present care for the marvellous monuments and objects of the past which lie within its jurisdiction.

Museums

No mention has yet been made of the two museums in the country: the official Jordan Archaeological Museum in Amman, which is part of the department, and the Palestine Archaeological Museum in Jerusalem, which is an independent body with its own income from an endowment fund. The government museum in Amman is a fairly recent venture, and is not yet fully arranged, but it has all the choicest pieces from excavations in Jordan during the past thirty years, as well as many other fine objects which have been acquired from those who found them casually. It is a comparatively small building, but most excellently planned for the purpose; the lighting is good even in the furthermost corners of the main hall and offices. The architect was Austen Harrison, who also designed the Palestine Archaeological Museum; the building of the latter was financed by John D.

Rockefeller, Jr., who also provided the endowment fund, and this generosity made possible the large and very fine structure, whereas the Amman Museum was built from the slender resources of the Jordan Government. Since the end of the Mandate the Jerusalem museum has been administered by an international board of trustees.

Even for those not interested in antiquities, the Palestine Archaeological Museum is well worth visiting from the architectural point of view, for it combined in a most happy manner the old indigenous type of cross-vault construction with modern techniques. Great thought and care were given to every detail of the building; the lettering in the various rooms is by Eric Gill, who also carved a series of panels which are set between the arches of the central court cloisters and represent the various peoples who influenced the growth and history of Palestine. The panel over the front door, depicting the meeting of Asia and Africa in Palestine, is also his work. The whole complex includes a lecture theater, workshops, laboratory, storerooms, photographic studios, library and administration offices in addition to the magnificent entrance hall and exhibition galleries.

The exhibits are arranged chronologically in the north and south galleries, starting with earliest prehistoric times in the south gallery and ending with the medieval Arab period in the north gallery. Behind each of these galleries are smaller ones where students can work and study the original objects. Gallery books, available to the visitor, give a brief history of the period concerned and a complete list of all the objects on display; in the cases the most important exhibits are indicated by a red star beside them.

The south gallery covers the period from about 200,000 years ago to the end of the Bronze Age, about 1300 B.C., and the north gallery carries on from the Iron Age, c. 1200 B.C., to A.D. 1700. In addition to these two main galleries there are other halls where special exhibitions are arranged; in the South Octagon can be seen some of the carved wooden panels and beam-covers which were found in the Aqsa Mosque when the interior was being remodelled some years ago. In the West Hall adjoining, carved stucco or plaster from the Umayyad palace at Jericho (Khirbat al Mafjar) is on show; the greater part of this has been reconstructed from thousands of small, broken fragments and has involved several years of patient work by the museum formatore. The results are astonishing, and give a vivid impression of the exuberance of decoration in the palace and baths, and of the fertile invention and imagination of the architects and sculptors responsible. In a small room between the West Hall and the North Octagon is an exhibition of jewelry of all periods, though the majority of it is Roman or Byzantine.

At the eastern end of the North Gallery a special temporary exhibition of the Dead Sea Scrolls has been set up, and most of the manuscripts which it has been possible to assemble and publish have been placed on show. There is also the pottery and other objects from the caves and the settlement at Qumran, and in a separate case the manuscripts and other finds from the caves at Murabbaat, including the letter of Bar Kochbar.

Adjoining this exhibition on the north a complete tomb of the Hyksos period from Jericho (about 1600 B.C.) has been reconstructed exactly as found. Here can be seen the remains of the wooden tables, stools and boxes with bone inlay, the baskets, scarabs, water jars and other pottery, and the remains of the funereal meats on dishes of pottery and wood, all laid out around the central body, which lies on a low bench with other skeletons around and behind him. In fact, it is just as the excavators of Jericho saw it when they removed the stone plug from the entrance for the first time in thirty-five hundred years.

The entrance hall and adjoining octagons contain a number of large objects and sculpture, and a small exhibition of recent acquisitions is often to be found there. The central courtyard (where are the Gill panels already referred to) has a rectangular lily pool, and at the west end a tiled alcove with a fountain, which, owing to the excessive cost of water, is now no longer kept playing. The pool is surrounded by cloisters on the other three sides, in which a number of monumental objects—such as marble sarcophagi—are set out.

The front garden of the museum is one of the sights of Jerusalem and makes a colorful foreground for the fine entrance, tower and main block of the building, which is all of white limestone. The garden has been carefully maintained despite constantly rising costs, and in spring the ground under the olive trees is covered with a wide variety of the wild flowers of the country, which have been collected over many years.

In a special part of the museum, the scholars work who are assembling, transcribing and translating the fragments of the Dead Sea Scrolls; they are an international team—English, French, American, Polish, German—and all are expert Semitic and Biblical scholars. Their task is one requiring infinite patience and enthusiasm, for they first have to soften and flatten out the bundles or screws of leather (the form in which the manuscripts often reach them), then sort through the thousands of fragments, bringing together those they believe to belong to the same manuscript, then try to fit the pieces together and eventually to read and translate what they have assembled. They are helped in their task by having every fragment photographed on infra-red film, which reveals any writing on pieces which to the naked eye appear to have merely a blank surface. This work has been going on now for several years, and there is still a great deal to be done; some of the most recent finds have scarcely been looked at as yet. But the scholars have lost none of their original enthusiasm for the task, and excitement always runs high when a new acquisition of fragments arrives. They gather round the dusty little pile of pieces of leather, feverishly yet with infinite care sorting them out, and each hoping to find some nice large piece which will fit into a manuscript on which he is already working.

The Palestine Archaeological Museum and its trustees have contributed considerably to the preservation of the Dead Sea Scrolls, both financially by buying fragments whenever possible and by providing accommodation and facilities for the work of the scholars. But finances have now been strained to their utmost, and it is only with the aid of a grant from John D. Rockefeller, Jr., that the scholars are able to continue with their work. Co-operation between the museum and the Department of Antiquities

193

has always been most cordial (the Director of Antiquities is a member of the board of trustees), and it is to be hoped that whatever the future of Jerusalem may be this happy state of affairs may continue, for both can be of the utmost assistance to each other. The museum, again, is fortunate at present in having for its curator a man who is completely devoted to his work and whose handling of all the problems involved, both administrative and personal, is guided by one principle only—the furtherance of archaeology and the greater glory of the museum. Given a continuance of present conditions, then, both the department and the Palestine Archaeological Museum have a great future before them.

Brief Comparative
Chronological Table

BRIEF COMPARATIVE CHRONOLOGICAL TABLE

Palaeolithic to Neolithic periods c. 100,000–4000 B.C.

Chalcolithic period c. 4000–3000 B.C.

Early Bronze Age c. 3000–2000 B.C.

MESOPOTAMIA	EGYPT	PALESTINE	EDOM	MOAB	AMMON	
Sumer and Accad	Dynasties I–XI					
Amorite and Hurrian Invasions	Dynasties XII to XVII. The Hyksos	Abraham; The Hyksos				Middle Bronze Age, c. 2000–1600 B.C.
Hurrians, Kassites. Rise of Assyria	Dynasties XVIII and XIX. Greatest period of Egyptian Empire	The Exodus, Moses, Joshua, Ehud	Bela; Jobab; Hushan	Balak	Sihon (at Heshbon)	Late Bronze Age, c. 1600–1200 B.C.
Assyrian Empire		Period of Judges and the Philistines	Hadad I; Samlah; Shaul	Eglon		Early Iron Age, c. 1200–950 B.C.
Tiglath Pileser I c. 1100 B.C.	Dynasties XX–XXI. Shishank I invaded Palestine 922 B.C.	Saul, 1020–1004 B.C.; David, 1004–965 B.C.; Solomon, 965–926 B.C.	Baal Hanan; Hadad II; Hadad III		Nahash; Hanun; Shobi	
		Israel — Omri, 882–871 · *Judah* — Jehoshaphat, 872–852	Shalman	Mesha, c. 850 B.C.	Sanibu	Late Iron Age, c. 950–549 B.C.
Tiglath Pileser III, 745–727	Dynasties XXII to XXVI	Menahem · Ahaz, 742–725	Melek Ram	Chemosh Nadab		
Sennacherib, 705–681		Fall of Samaria, 721 B.C. · Hezekiah, 725–697	Qaus Gaber	Chemosh Nadab	Pudiel	
		Manasseh, 696–642		Mutsuri		
		Amon, 641–640		Under Assyrian Rule		
Ashur-Bani-Pal, 669–626		Josiah, 639–609		Chemosh Yehi	Ammi Nadab	

Babylonian Empire Nebuchadnezzar, 605–562

Zedekiah, 598–587
Fall of Jerusalem, 587 B.C. Exile

Chemosh Haleth

Persian Empire, 549–331 B.C.

Return of the Jews

Persian period, 549–331 B.C.

Alexander the Great, c. 333 B.C.

Hellenistic period, 331–63 B.C.

Baalis

Tobias

Seleucid Kingdom in Syria } Ptolemaic Dynasties

Petty local rulers under the Ptolemies and Seleucids

Nabataean Kingdom

Fluctuating between Jewish, Ptolemaic, Seleucid and Nabataean control

Aretas I, c. 169 B.C.
Aretas II, 110–96
Obodas I, 95–90
Rabel I, 90–87
Aretas III, 87–62
Obodas II, 62–47
Malichus II, 47–30
Obodas III, 30–9
Aretas IV, 9 B.C.–A.D. 40
Malichus III, A.D. 40–75
Rabel II, A.D. 75–106

Rise of the Roman Empire, c. 62 B.C.

Roman period, 62 B.C. to A.D. 330

Herod the Great
First Jewish Revolt

Whole country subdued by the Romans, A.D. 106

Second Jewish Revolt

Byzantine Empire, A.D. 330–640

Arab Conquest, A.D. 640

197

Index

The Arabic article "al" is disregarded in the arrangement of subjects in alphabetical order.

198

Jarash (*continued*)

Nymphaeum, 70, 78, 79; South Gate, 74, 75; South Tetrapylon, 67, 72, 74, 78-9; South theater, 69, 76, 77; Street of Columns, 78, 83, 109; temples of Artemis, 68, 69, 70, 73, 74, 79-82, 88; temple of Dionysos, 85; temples of Zeus, 67-8, 69, 70, 76, 77-8, 88; Triumphal Arch, 74, 75

Christian and Byzantine monuments: cathedral, 72, 79, 84-5, 136; churches, 72, 73-4, 84-5, 89; churches of St. John, St. George, SS. Cosmos and Damian, 87-9; Church of the Prophets, Apostles and Martyrs, 72, 89; Church of St. Theodore, 72, 73, 85, 86-7; Fountain Court, 72; Viaduct Church, 80

Jarash-Ajlun road, 42
Jarash-Husn road, 2, 41
Jason, high priest of Jerusalem, 107
Jazirat Firaun, 127
Jehoiakim, king of Judah, 30
Jehoram, king of Israel, 27, 94
Jehoshaphat, king of Judah, 25-6, 27, 94
Jehovah, 61, 104-5
Jephthah, 23
Jeremiah, 50
Jericho: excavations, 13, 151; exhibits in Palestine Archaeological Museum, 192; and stones of Mafjar, 162; today, 164-5

prehistory and history: Neolithic, 13-14, 152-5; Chalcolithic, 155; Bronze Age, 155-9; Iron Age and after, 160; defeat of Moabites at, 22; Herod at, 176; tenth legion at, 178

Jerusalem, 9, 42, 49, 50, 58, 91, 92, 150, 175; Church of Holy Sepulcher, 162; rebuilding the temple, 31; sixth century picture of, 58. See also École Biblique et Archaeologique Française; Palestine Archaeological Museum

Jerusalem-Amman road, 1
Jewish revolts: A.D. 66, 177-8; A.D. 132-5, 178
Jewish war, A.D. 70, 77
Jiza, 148

Joab, 24, 48-9
Jogbehah (Jubaihah), 23
John the Baptist, 34, 90
Jordan: agriculture, 3, 7; climate, 3-4; description, 1-3; fauna, 5-6; flora, 4-5; foreign influences, early, 10-11; frontier, 124; in geological times, 12; highest point, 98; inhabitants, 6-8; insects, 4; map, facing p. 1; religion, 8-9

prehistory: Palaeolithic, 12-13; Neolithic, 13-14; Chalcolithic, 14-15; Bronze Age, 15-21

history: Biblical accounts, 18-21; and Israelites, 21; Iron Age, 21-31; and Babylon, 30; and Persia, 31; in Hellenistic times, 31-3; in Roman and Byzantine times, 33-5; sixth century map of, 74; under the Arabs, 35-6; under the Turks, 36; and British mandate, 36-7; as the Hashemite Kingdom, 37

See also Antiquities Law; Department of Antiquities

Jordan Archaeological Museum, 9, 190f
Jordan River, 1, 23, 24, 162
Jordan valley, 1, 4, 11, 20, 42, 129; view of, 40, 42, 61; Neolithic culture in, 13, 14; Chalcolithic site in, 14; Umayyad palaces in, 162; road from, 83
Josephus, 51, 67, 176; on the Essenes, 178; *Antiquities of the Jews*, 56
Joshua, 21; attack on Jericho, 160
Jotham, king, seal of, 28
Jovian, emperor, 140
Jubaihah, 23
Judea, 178
Judas Maccabeus, 32
Julia Domna, 82
Jurf al Darawish, 97
Justinian, emperor, 72, 88

Kadesh, 19
Kafrinji, 44
Kanatha (Kanawat), 33
Karak, 20, 27, 34, 35, 36, 42, 43, 57, 58, 91, 94-6
Karkur, 23
Kenyon, Dr. Kathleen, 151, 154n

Nabataeans (*continued*)
dom, 33, *107*; and Amman, 51,
107; and Pompey, 33; and Mark
Antony, 108; and Herod the
Great, 34, 108; and Herod the
Tetrarch, 34, 108; kingdom
broken up, 34; and Rome, 69,
108
inscriptions: at Jabal Rum, 130; at
Jarash, 68; at Ras al Naqab, 123;
at Umm al Jamal, 134, 136
remains: at Dhiban, 92; at Jabal
Rum, 129-30; at Karak, 95; at
Khirbat al Khaldi, 124-5; at
Khirbat al Tannur, 11, 96-7; at
Petra, 109-20, 130; at Al Qasr,
93; at Qasr al Hallabat, 138; at
Quairah, 124; at Umm al Jamal,
133; in Wadi Rum, 127-31
Nahash, king of Ammon, 23, 24, 48,
49
Najal, 98
Nasir, Sultan, 127
Naur, 16, 17
Nazareth, 38
Nebo, 26
Nebo, Mount, 16, 21, 59-61
Nebuchadnezzar, king of Babylon,
30, 50
Neolithic man, 152
Nero, emperor, 108
Nuaimah, 162

Obodas I, king of Nabataeans, 107
Obodas III, king of Nabataeans, 108
Og, king of Bashan, 20, 47
Olives, Mount of, 61
Omar, caliph, 127
Omri, king of Israel, 26, 27
Oreb, prince of Midian, 23
Oultre Jourdain, 94

Pakidas, a god, 68
Palestine, 10, 11, 16-32 passim, 37,
46, 107, 156, 158, 159, 172, 176,
187; mosaic map of, 58; view of,
118
Palestine Archaeological Museum,
159, 168, 173, 190-93
Palestine mandate, 36, 37
Palestine Tertia, 51
Palestinians, 8; refugees, 150-51
Palmyra, 63, 71
204

Parthians, 108
Pasebkhanu, pharaoh, 24
Paul, St., 108
Payem, lord of Karak, 94
Pella (Tabaqat Fahil), 33
Penuel, 23
Peor, 21
Peraea, 34
Perdiccas, 67
Persia, 31
Persian invasion, A.D. 614, 35, 73
Peter the Iberian, 59-60
Petra, 9, 11, 63, 127, 129; approach
to, 98; climate, 3-4; excursion
from Beirut, 99; ornithology, 5;
plan of, 110; prehistory, 103;
rediscovery, 100-102, today, 99-
100
in Biblical times, 103; as Sela, and
Amaziah, 27; and the Nabataeans,
103; Diodorus on, 105; Strabo
on, 106-7
later history: Greco-Syrian attacks, 105-6; from c120 B.C. to
A.D. 106, 107-8; as a Roman city,
34, 108-9; bishoprics, 51, 109
monuments, 116-17; Corinthian
tomb, 115; Al Dair, 117-18; High
Place of Sacrifice, 117, 118-20;
houses, 120; El Khaznah, 111-12,
115; palace tomb, 115; Qasr al
Bint, 113-14; Roman soldier,
tomb of, 118; Sextus Florentinus,
tomb of, 115; snake monument,
117; the Syk, 111; theater, 112;
tombs, 109, 120; tomb with
Nabataean inscription, 116; Urn
tomb, 114-15
Petra-Amman road, 57
Petra-Maan road, 122-3
Philadelphia (Amman), 32, 33, 51,
65
Phoenician influence, 28
Pigeon post in Arab empire, 43
Pisgah, 21, 61
Placcus, bishop of Jarash, 72, 73, 87
Pliny the Elder, 179
Pompey, 33, 67, 68, 107
Potter's wheel, Jericho, 158
Pottery: archaeological significance
of, 14; in Jordan, Chalcolithic,
15; Early Bronze Age, 15; Middle
Bronze, 16; Late Bronze, 17, 22;

205